Dr Graham MacGregor is Professor of Cardiovascular Medicine and Honorary Consultant Physician at St George's Hospital Medical School in London. He is Director of the Blood Pressure Unit at St George's Hospital and has many years' experience of treating patients with high blood pressure. His major research interest has been into the mechanisms involved in the development of high blood pressure and, in particular, the role of salt. The Blood Pressure Unit was the first to demonstrate unequivocally that moderate reduction of salt intake does lower blood pressure in many patients with high blood pressure.

O P T I M A

THE LOW-SALT DIET BOOK

Christiane & Graham MacGregor

POSITIVE HEALTH GUIDE

© Graham MacGregor, 1984

First published in the United Kingdom in 1984
by Martin Dunitz Ltd, 154 Camden High Street, London NW1 0NE

This edition published in 1991 by
Macdonald Optima, a division of
Macdonald & Co. (Publishers) Ltd
A member of Maxwell Macmillan Pergamon Publishing Corporation plc

British Library Cataloguing in Publication Data

MacGregor, Graham
  The low-salt diet book.—2nd. ed.
  1. Food : Low salt dishes — Recipes
  I. Title II. Series
  641.5632

  ISBN 0-356-19774-3

Macdonald & Co. (Publishers) Ltd
Orbit House
1 New Fetter Lane
London EC4A 1AR

Front cover *photograph shows: Leeks vinaigrette (top, see page 50), Chilli con carne (centre right, see page 74), Spaghetti with ground basil sauce (bottom, see page 51).*

CONTENTS

INTRODUCTION
Who needs a low-salt diet?

Nutritional experts throughout the world are now recommending a reduction in salt intake for the whole population and particularly for those people who have high blood pressure. High blood pressure leads to strokes and heart attacks and is probably one of the most preventable causes of death in the Western world.

This book explains how salt in small amounts is necessary in our bodies and how too much can be harmful for those who already have high blood pressure or heart problems and perhaps for healthy people too. There are many ways of cutting down your salt intake but it is really easy when you know where the salt is in the food you eat.

The first part of the book shows what quantities you should be aiming for and how it can be done. You will soon learn to enjoy the taste of less salty, but attractively flavoured foods. The recipes were developed on this basis and as you try them out, you will find that the real reason to reduce your salt intake is that natural good food tastes better without it.

Salt – what is it?

Although salt is the chemical name for many substances made up of crystals, when the word salt is mentioned we all think of table salt or the salt that is put on the roads, and that is of course the type we are describing in the book. Known as sodium chloride, it is made up of approximately 40 per cent sodium and 60 per cent chloride. Salt is the main source of sodium in the Western diet, but some other foods contain it in other forms, for example, the sodium bicarbonate in baking powder, which is used in baking biscuits and cakes. But for simplicity many people refer to salt when in fact they mean sodium, and vice versa.

Sodium's vital role in the body

All the cells that make up our body are bathed in a fluid which contains sodium and chloride in solution, that is, a salt solution. The concentration of sodium in this fluid is very carefully regulated by the body and is approximately the same as the sodium that was in the sea when life emerged on to land many millions of years ago. The sea now contains more sodium because of erosion of the land by rain over the last few million years, which has washed sodium down into the sea. Sodium and chloride are vital for both the working of the body cells and in regulating the volume of blood and fluid around them.

The body is made up of millions of little cells surrounded by fluid containing sodium. Inside these cells there is very little sodium whereas there is a large amount of another mineral, potassium. The outer covering or membrane of the cell allows both potassium and sodium to pass through it. As sodium is in much greater concentration outside the cell, there is a continuous tendency for it to move in and, as potassium is in a greater concentration inside the cell, there is a tendency for it to come out. To maintain the balance between sodium outside the cell and potassium inside, there is a sodium-potassium pump on the membrane which is continuously pumping sodium out as potassium is pumped into the cell.

Fluid retention

The amount of sodium in your body affects the volume of fluid bathing the tissues. If a large amount of sodium is eaten the body retains some of it and water stays with it, so that the volume of fluid in the body increases. This can be clearly seen if you increase sodium intake from a very low amount, say 10 mmol (0.25 g) per day, to a high amount of about 250 mmol (6 g) per day (see page 22 for an explanation of measurements). The increase in sodium intake causes fluid retention, making a weight gain of around 1½ kg (3 lb). A reduction of sodium intake from a very high level to a low level will cause a loss of sodium and therefore of water. With this fluid loss there will be a loss of weight. Many weight-reducing diets use this principle. For instance, if you do not eat for a few days, or you eat food with no sodium, there will be an initial loss of weight, which is due to loss of body fluid, which is immediately regained if more sodium is eaten.

How do we regulate the sodium content of the body?

The amount of sodium in the body is a balance between the amount eaten, nearly all of which is absorbed into the body, and the amount excreted by the kidneys into the urine. When we eat more sodium there is an increase both in the sodium and the fluid inside the body until the body's mechanisms, mainly regulated by hormones (messengers in the blood), come in. They cause loss of more sodium in the urine and a new balance is obtained at a slightly higher fluid level in the whole body.

How much sodium or salt do we actually need?

During evolution and even in some societies today, humans were dependent for sodium on the very low amount in fruits and vegetables and the occasional meal of meat or fish, which had a slightly higher sodium content. Clearly, we were able to survive on this very low sodium diet mainly because of the kidney's great ability to hold on to sodium when it is in short supply in the diet. Studies on Indian tribes in the Venezuelan jungle have shown how well we are adapted to a very low sodium diet. Measurement of these tribes and estimates of our ancestors over the last million years indicate that natural sodium intake is approximately between 0.5 and 10 mmol per day (10 to 250 mg per day).

With increasing civilization, salt could be obtained either by evaporating sea water or by mining it. It was found that it had the almost magical property of preserving food. This was particularly important in the winter and, not surprisingly, salt which had nearly always been in short supply, became highly valued. Indeed, Roman soldiers were partly paid in salt, hence the word 'salary'. At the same time as preserving food, salt was thought to purify it, and for this reason it took on religious as well as economic importance.

With our recent ability to produce salt very cheaply, and since we've found other ways of preserving food, its value has lessened considerably, although as a chemical salt is still very important.

Sodium is often in short supply in animals and more primitive human communities, and they have a strong salt appetite seen, for example, in deer or cattle going to salt licks. In the West our sodium intake is so high that we have no such craving for salt. But as a result of habit, we have become used to eating a very large amount. The average consumption of sodium in the West is around 120 to 250 mmol of sodium per day, or 8 to 14 g of sodium chloride per day (for a fuller explanation of how sodium is measured see page 22). There is now general agreement that this is far too much.

The very low amounts of sodium eaten by primitive man are not, at the present time, practical in the West unless tremendous care is taken with the diet. Even if they were, an intake of around 1 mmol per day could be dangerous if there was a big loss of body fluids due to diarrhoea or severe vomiting. However, most experts would agree that cutting the amount by about half to around 50 to 80 mmol of sodium per day would be a sensible compromise for the present. Remember that this is at least five times more than was eaten during the last million years of our evolution. Once you know how, it is relatively easy to reduce your sodium intake to this amount and, in our experience, most people taking the diet up have found it a lot more enjoyable than their previous high-salt diet.

Why is too much salt harmful?

A high-salt consumption can be harmful in several conditions, but by far the most important effect is on blood pressure, and this may lead to serious disease.

High blood pressure

Six out of ten of us will die from some disorder of the small blood vessels that supply oxygen and essential nutrients to the tissues. These small blood vessels called arteries, and the even smaller ones, which are called arterioles, become narrowed and scarred with fatty deposits as we grow older. This is known as atheroma or arteriosclerosis. The scarring and narrowing of the arteries is directly responsible for strokes or cerebrovascular accidents, heart attacks and some forms of kidney disease. Arterial disease may also affect arteries in the limbs and in particular the blood supply to the legs.

Clearly, an understanding of the cause of this arterial disease would result in a major improvement in health and an increase in life expectancy. Studies from all over the world looking at different communities have shown that there are three important factors that make it much more likely for someone to develop arterial disease and therefore to die of a stroke or heart attack. These are:

1. High blood pressure
2. High saturated fat intake (leading to increased blood cholesterol)
3. Smoking

What is blood pressure?

This is the pressure of the blood in the arteries. Blood is pumped through the arteries, capillaries and veins by the heart contracting. When the heart contracts the pressure of the blood in the arteries rises to a peak, called the systolic pressure, and when the heart relaxes the pressure in the arteries falls but not down to zero because the arteries are elastic and have some recoil. This lower pressure when the heart is relaxed is known as diastolic pressure.

How is it measured?

Blood pressure can be measured in any artery in the body but the easiest way is with a cuff that can be inflated around the arm. The cuff is filled with air to a pressure above the pressure of blood in the artery so that no blood goes into the lower arm. Then the cuff is slowly deflated and blood flows back into the arm. Measurement is by a column of mercury expressed as the height of the column in millimetres (mmHg). At the systolic pressure the flow in the artery will be disturbed by the cuff and sounds will be heard through the stethoscope. Systolic pressure can be more easily, but less accurately, measured by feeling for the pulse beat as the cuff is deflated.

Systolic pressure can be more easily, but less accurately, measured by feeling for the pulse beat as the cuff is deflated.

When the pressure of the cuff reaches diastolic pressure, the flow in the arteries is less disturbed and the sounds heard with the stethoscope disappear, so we are able to measure the diastolic pressure as well.

What is a normal blood pressure?
Everyone's blood pressure varies. For instance, it is lowest during sleep, when the muscles are relaxed, and high during mental or physical activity or periods of anxiety. It even varies according to whether you're standing or sitting. In relaxed conditions, for an average person, a systolic pressure above 160 mmHg or a diastolic pressure above 90 mmHg is said to be abnormal. We write this as 160/90 mmHg. Using this measurement, around 20 per cent or one person in five of the population in the West has high blood pressure.

How do you know if you have high blood pressure?
There are no symptoms. The only way of knowing what your blood pressure is, is to have it measured. If you do not know it, why not have it checked? Knowing it is a lot more important than knowing your weight. Keeping your blood pressure down will largely prevent the far too common complications of high blood pressure, particularly strokes.

How does salt raise blood pressure?
Studies in animals have shown that the higher the salt intake, the higher the blood pressure. As it is not possible to do similar experiments on humans we have to rely on more circumstantial evidence from studying different communities. Comparing salt intake in primitive communities, where very little sodium is eaten, with countries in the West, where much more sodium is eaten, has shown that there is a direct relationship between salt intake in a particular community and the number of people in that community with high blood pressure. The table below gives an idea of the levels in the different communities.

There is general agreement that in the majority of people who are going to develop or have developed high blood pressure, there is an inherited abnormality of the kidney which is responsible. But the effect of this abnormality has been a puzzle for some time. It could be that there is a difficulty is getting rid of sodium. If this

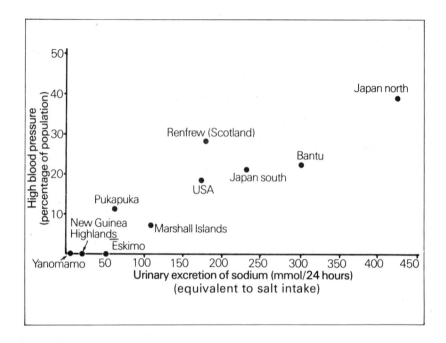

were so, people with high blood pressure on a high-sodium diet would retain slightly more fluid inside the body, and some years ago this was thought by many to be a cause of high blood pressure. But as we now know, the majority of people with high blood pressure have the same amount of fluid in the blood and around their tissues as people with normal blood pressure, so an increase in fluid could not be the direct cause.

A more recent suggestion is that the defect in the kidney's ability to get rid of sodium causes an increase in a sodium excreting hormone in an attempt to overcome the abnormality. It would seem that this increased sodium excreting hormone is largely successful in getting rid of the extra sodium in the body but as a side effect it might slow down sodium pumps, not only in the kidney but also in the cell membranes, particularly in the little cells surrounding the arterioles, which are more contracted in people with high blood pressure. There is now some evidence to support this theory: the pumps are slower in people with high blood pressure. When the sodium pumps are slowed the cells around the arteries contract and the arteries narrow. The result is a greater resistance to flow, and after a while there is a rise in the pressure of blood trying to move into these little arteries. High blood pressure seems therefore to be caused both by an inherited abnormality of the kidney and, more importantly as it can be changed, the amount of sodium or salt in the diet.

Does reducing sodium intake prevent the development of high blood pressure? Tests on animals that would normally develop high blood pressure show a reduction of sodium intake will nearly always prevent the condition. There have been no similar tests done on humans and such evidence is unlikely to be available for many years; although one study on newborn babies done in Holland in 1983 showed that a group fed on a low sodium diet for one year had lower blood pressure than a similar group fed on a normal sodium diet. Doctors now generally agree that people who have a family history of high blood pressure, strokes and heart attacks should cut back on their sodium intake as this group particularly is at risk.

Does reducing sodium intake lower blood pressure when it is already raised? There is no doubt that this is so. About forty years ago, before tablets were developed, high blood pressure was treated by cutting out salt almost entirely. Very low sodium diets were effective but many people found them monotonous and difficult to stick to. Much more exciting is the recent realization that a less drastic reduction of sodium, to around half of what we now eat, does lower blood pressure to about the same extent as taking a single blood pressure lowering tablet each day. Although this does not always cure blood pressure when it is already raised, it can be very helpful even for people with mildly raised blood pressure, when tablets are not considered necessary.

Other studies have also shown that cutting sodium intake by half greatly improves the action of blood pressure lowering tablets if you are already on them.

If you have high blood pressure and you do decide to cut back on your sodium intake, it is a good idea to discuss this with your doctor. In some people, particularly those on a very high sodium intake, it may have a marked blood pressure lowering effect and it may sometimes be possible to stop one of the tablets that you are on, particularly the diuretic tablets, but this should never be done without consulting your doctor.

What else can you do if you have high blood pressure?

WEIGHT

Many studies have shown that if you are overweight and you reduce your weight to normal, this will cause the blood pressure to fall.

SMOKING

If you smoke, it is extremely important to stop. This will, in itself, reduce the risk of a heart attack and to a lesser extent, the risk of a stroke, as well as reducing the danger of developing lung cancer.

ALCOHOL

Excessive amounts of alcohol have been shown to increase blood pressure very considerably, particularly the day after drinking large quantities. It is sensible therefore to not drink excessively. Intake should be restricted to an average of one to two drinks a day, that is, ¼ to ½ a litre (½ to 1 pint) of beer, one to two glasses of wine or one to two measures of spirits.

POTASSIUM

Increasing potassium intake may lower blood pressure and as potassium is mainly present in fruit and vegetables it is a good idea to increase consumption of these foods. Besides, eating more fruit and vegetables helps to reduce sodium intake and at the same time decreases the amount of saturated fat in the diet, as well as increasing the fibre content. (For further details on potassium, see page 28.)

FAT

All nutritional experts recommend a reduction in total fat intake, and a switch from saturated fats (mainly but not invariably animal fat) to fats rich in polyunsaturates, eg, corn oil, sunflower oil (see page 29), or monosaturated fats, eg, olive oil.

EXERCISE

Regular exercise or keeping fit makes you feel better and may lower blood pressure.

The usual assumption is that the more relaxed you are, the lower your blood pressure will be. There is no doubt that when you are asleep your blood pressure falls (see page 13). Your muscles relax and the pressure drops. Most relaxation techniques such as biofeedback, yoga and meditation are based on this physiological reflex and may lower blood pressure during the relaxation.

However, we are not able to say for certain that blood pressure is lower after you have finished a period of relaxation, and there is no direct evidence that a hectic, stressed lifestyle contributes directly to the cause of high blood pressure.

Sodium intake in other situations

While high blood pressure is the biggest danger to people eating a lot of salt, there are other reasons that make cutting down important, even in the youngest age groups.

Babies and young children

The kidneys of young babies are not able to handle the amounts of sodium that adults can. In the 1960s, powdered milk for feeding babies contained too much sodium. Many were at risk from developing a high level of sodium in the fluid around their tissues. Fortunately, this was realized and the amount of sodium in powdered milk was reduced, although even now, when properly made up, it still contains more sodium than human milk. At the same time as the amount of sodium in powdered milk was reduced, so was the quantity in baby foods. But recent studies have shown that mothers often make the dried milk too concentrated, and in preparing other foods for babies they tend to add salt to their own taste and end up with a diet that contains more sodium than the manufactured food. It is very important to follow the instructions exactly when making up dried milk and not to use too much. You should not add salt to food that is being prepared for babies.

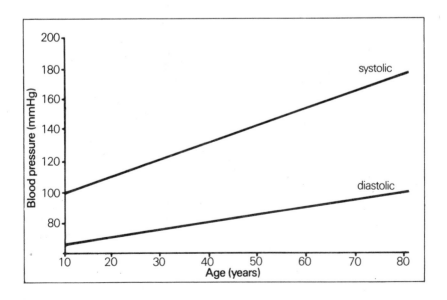

Most pre-school and young schoolchildren are eating foods with a very high sodium content. Many young children exist almost entirely on processed snacks and other foods very high in sodium – and fat – for example, potato chips, biscuits and burgers. The food that children eat largely determines the food they eat later in life. There is great concern amongst many nutritionists that the next generation, because of the much higher sodium intake that they become used to at a young age, will produce an even greater number of people with high blood pressure than in the present adult population. Certainly, it would be a good idea to guide our children to eat a more healthy diet, particularly to eat more fresh fruit and vegetables rather than the processed snacks, sweets and fast foods that they eat so often now.

Sodium and premenstrual swelling

Nearly all women have experienced a gain in weight and a feeling of bloatedness before their periods. Many get these symptoms at other times. The exact cause of this retention of sodium and water is not clear, although the premenstrual swelling is likely to be due to the hormonal changes that occur during the menstrual cycle. The most common symptoms are a bloated feeling, swelling of the abdomen and sometimes swelling of the ankles and fingers, particularly noticed on the ring fingers. If these symptoms are bad, women are treated with diuretics. These cause the kidney to lose more sodium and water. The swelling will temporarily go down. Unfortunately, these tablets have many longterm side effects and do, though rarely, cause such conditions as diabetes and gout. More importantly, they only temporarily relieve the swelling. At times they can actually increase it by making the body try to compensate so that when the water tablet is stopped, there is greater retention of sodium and water. This often leads to a vicious circle where women are advised by their doctor to stop the water tablets (diuretics) but find that as soon as they do, they swell up badly. This can give the mistaken idea that they really need these pills.

A more logical way of treating any swelling of this kind is to reduce the amount of salt or sodium in the diet. The less sodium you eat, the less fluid will be locked into the body. As well as cutting back on salt, another helpful move is to eat more potassium as this helps the body to get rid of sodium and so lose the extra fluid (see pages 14, 28). Our experience with women who have very bad swelling and who have been on diuretic pills for many years is that if they restrict their sodium intake, following the ways outlined in this book, and at the same time increase their potassium intake, particularly by eating more fresh fruit and vegetables, they can keep all the problems of swelling to the minimum. Why not try it? You may be surprised at how effective this diet is.

Remember that another important factor in the retention of sodium and water is varying your eating, particularly changing your sodium and carbohydrate intake. Many people try to lose weight by crash dieting. Often, they fast effectively for several days and then go out and have a large meal. This causes great retention of sodium and therefore water, so that they swell up. If you want to lose weight, it is much more sensible to reduce food intake over a long period and get used to eating less food. It is important to take regular meals rather than trying a crash diet followed by bingeing.

Sodium and heart failure

The heart pumps the blood around the body. If the arteries to the heart are narrowed, this can cause damage to the muscle of the heart, and it is then not able to pump properly. When this happens, the kidney retains more sodium and water to try and help the heart pump better; but this fluid retention unfortunately often makes the heart pump less well. Water tablets are given to get rid of the extra sodium and water. Another way is to restrict the amount of sodium in the diet, sometimes along with, and sometimes instead of taking the pills. Many studies have shown that this can be very helpful.

If you have heart failure and feel that you would like to try cutting down on sodium, you must discuss it with your doctor. Many people who do cut back on their sodium intake will find that they will be able to reduce the dose of the tablets, but do need proper medical advice about this.

Sodium and liver disease

When the liver is damaged the kidney may retain sodium and water, leading to swelling, and so again cutting back on sodium intake in the diet can be of great help. As with heart failure, it is very important if you have liver disease to discuss this first with your doctor. It may well be necessary to adjust your dose of diuretics.

Sodium and kidney disease

The kidney is an extremely important organ that not only controls the amount of sodium in the body but also gets rid of impurities from the blood. In some illnesses where the kidney stops working properly, its ability to get rid of sodium is reduced, often causing high blood pressure. Reducing sodium intake can be helpful in reducing the blood pressure. However, if the kidney is badly affected, a severe reduction in sodium intake may impair the working of the kidney more.

In another form of kidney disease, where protein is lost in the urine, the so-called 'nephrotic syndrome', there is retention by the kidney of sodium and water, often with very great swelling. Water tablets are nearly always needed to control the swelling, but reduction in sodium intake can also be very helpful in controlling the swelling. This often means that a lower dose of the water tablets can be taken.

In some very rare forms of kidney disease the kidney is unable to hold on to sodium and there is a loss of sodium from the body, and so it may be dangerous to cut back on sodium intake. It is vital if you have kidney disease to discuss with your doctor whether it is a good idea for you to reduce your salt intake.

Should we all cut back on sodium intake?

There is much circumstantial evidence to suggest that if we cut back on sodium intake over a generation it would lower everyone's blood pressure rather than just those who have high blood pressure. If it did, it would reduce the chances of stroke and heart attacks, so improving the general health of the whole population. The animal studies show that it is very important that sodium intake should be restricted from the first years of life. We also know that even if your pressure is in the normal range but at the higher end your chances of reaching the high blood pressure area as you grow older are greater (see the diagram on page 17).

Decisions on public health have often been taken as a result of educated guesses in the face of an epidemic although there was no absolute proof of the cause. For example, vaccination for smallpox, and the provision of clean water and drainage at the time of the typhoid and cholera epidemics in Europe in the nineteenth century were introduced in these circumstances. Some of these changes were opposed by the medical profession at the time and evidence that they were beneficial came only after they were made. Most countries are now recommending a general reduction in sodium intake for the whole community rather than just for those with high blood pressure.

Are there any dangers to reducing sodium intake?

If you stick rigidly to the diet suggested in this book, you will be eating approximately 25 mmol (600 mg) of sodium per day. If you stick to it less rigidly your sodium intake will be around 50 to 80 mmol (1500 mg) per day. That is probably half of what you are now eating. Nevertheless, these amounts are three to ten times the quantities eaten by humans over the last million years and still eaten in many communities in the world at the present time.

There are two rare conditions where cutting your salt intake could possibly be harmful: first, in Addison's disease, when the adrenal gland (situated above the kidneys) fails. The adrenal gland secretes hormones that regulate the amount of sodium in the body. When the gland fails the body loses sodium, which can cause a loss of fluid around the body cells. Second, in some forms of kidney disease the kidney is not able to hold on to sodium (see page 19). If there's any chance of you having either condition, or if you are in any doubt, do consult your doctor before reducing your sodium intake.

Measuring salt or sodium intake

The average salt intake at the present time in the West is around 8 to 12 g per day, that is, about two teaspoonfuls. The aim is to reduce this by at least half. When measuring the salt (sodium chloride) intake, it is the sodium content that we are concerned with. In the UK and Australia the sodium intake is usually measured in millimoles, i.e., one-thousandth of a mole (a scientific unit of measurement for comparing different substances); in North America the measurement is in grams. When sodium levels are expressed in mmol, we can make comparisons with amounts of other molecules in the body. The conversion of grams to these Standard International Units is:

> 1 g of sodium chloride = 17.1 mmol of sodium
> 1 g of sodium = 43.5 mmol of sodium
> 1 g of potassium chloride = 13.4 mmol of potassium
> 1 g of potassium = 25.6 mmol of potassium
>
> NB 1 gram = 1000 milligrams

If the average sodium intake is 8 to 12 g per day, this will come out in mmols of sodium as 136 to 205 mmol per day. As this is a more modern way of measuring sodium, we have used mmols throughout the book, but in the recipes you will find the equivalent amount in milligrams (one-thousandth of a gram) of sodium as well. It does not really matter if you do not understand exactly what a mmol means as all that is important is knowing that the total amount on a normal Western diet ranges from 120 to 250 mmol per day and on a very low sodium diet it is around 10 mmol per day and what we are aiming for is to reduce sodium intake to between 50 to 80 mmol per day.

By calculating from the tables on pages 98–106 and the recipes the amount of sodium in the different foods that you eat, you can come up roughly with the amount of sodium that you are eating per day.

The most accurate way of measuring sodium intake is to record the amount coming out in the urine. This is not something you can do at home, nor is it necessary, but if you are being tested at a hospital, this is how it will be done.

How do you go about reducing sodium intake?

There are four important simple steps:

1. *Remove the salt cellar from the table.* This is no hardship; 10 to 50 per cent of your salt intake comes from the salt added at the table, yet studies done in Australia showed that when the hole in the salt cellar was half the normal size, people added half the quantity of salt to their food.

2. *Stop adding salt to cooking.* To begin with, food that you cook will taste rather bland but allow your taste receptors to adjust over a few weeks.

3. Avoid foods that have had sodium or salt added – usually these are processed foods. By using more natural foods such as fresh meat, fish, fruit and vegetables, you will straightaway be on a fairly low-sodium diet.

    However, some processed foods are allowed, depending on their sodium content (see detailed table of foods, page 98).

4. Look at the recipe section in this book for ideas on making food really wholesome. Remember, you can use your own recipes as well as long as you do not use table salt or any of the other sodium salts in them, and avoid the high-salt processed foods (beware of misleadingly labelled 'low-sodium' salts; for more on this, see page 28).

What problems are there on a low-sodium diet?

The initial bland taste of food   The salty taste of food is sensed by receptors on the tongue and mouth. The sensitivity of these receptors is reduced by increasing the amount of salt in the diet. On the high-salt diet that is at present eaten in the West, these receptors need very large amounts of sodium to notice a salty taste. However, once you have adjusted to a low-sodium diet, very small amounts of sodium produce a better salty taste. This adjustment in the salt-taste receptors does take time, anything from two to six weeks. Do not be surprised when you reduce your salt intake that food will start by tasting bland. Allow your taste receptors to adjust. When people stop adding large amounts of sugar to tea or coffee, similarly they find it difficult, but once adjusted, they realize that there are a lot of subtle flavours to different coffees and teas that they never appreciated before.

Natural foods have their own subtle flavours and can be varied by using flavours other than salt (see page 31). On a low-salt diet you will find that you become very much more discerning in distinguishing between different foods.

High-salt foods become unpleasant   Once adjusted to a low-sodium diet, you will find some of the very high salt foods you used to eat unpleasant.

The problem of processed foods   Most processed and prepared convenience foods have had sodium added in quite large amounts. Sticking to a low-sodium diet will mean giving up these particular foods. This can be difficult for people who don't have much time to prepare food and want to use convenience foods. Even worse in this respect are snack foods or ready-prepared meals.

The problem is exacerbated as most packaged foods do not give the quantity of sodium they contain, although some more progressive food manufacturers have started labelling their food with the sodium content. Obviously, the more pressure that is brought to bear, the quicker this will be done for all such foods. If your favourite food is not properly labelled, you could help by writing to the manufacturer about it yourself.

Eating out in restaurants   If you have been recommended a low-salt diet or have decided yourself to stick rigidly to one, you must choose your restaurant carefully. You are less able to control the salt content of your food than at home. As fast and convenience foods generally contain very large amounts of sodium – a well-known brand of hamburger and chips contains almost 100 mmol (6 g) of sodium, as does a well-known brand of fried chicken – avoid fast-food eating places. Much Chinese and Japanese food has large amounts of sodium added, not only as salt but also as monosodium glutamate, so you will have to forego or drastically reduce this sort of food too. Even in restaurants offering freshly cooked foods, the sodium content will depend first on the type of food and second on the chef. But here you should be able to select foods that are lower in sodium and some hotels and restaurants will prepare low-sodium foods if given notice in advance. Some restaurants cook dishes to order, such as omelettes, beefburgers, grilled steaks and fish, kebabs and tandoori chicken, so you can request them at least without added salt. Again, the more pressure that is brought to bear, the quicker restaurants and hotels will begin to cater for people who wish to cut back on their salt intake.

With friends   You will have to be tactful. With people you know well and who do their own cooking, it is a good idea to say beforehand that you are now on a low-salt diet.

Salt in our present diet

We can get a better understanding of how to restrict sodium intake in the diet by looking at exactly how the sodium content of our present diet is made up.

Added salt   Ten to 40 per cent of salt intake is added either at the table or in the cooking. It is important to remember that salt is not only present in table salt, but in all other forms – cooking salt, rock salt, sea salt, herb salt, garlic salt, and in other flavourings such as gravy browning, tomato paste, etc.

Processed food   Processed food usually contains large amounts of sodium or salt and can make up anything from 20 to 70 per cent of salt intake. Sodium is added to processed food for several reasons:

● Flavour: the processing of food often removes the natural taste. In order to restore it, sodium chloride and monosodium glutamate are added as flavour enhancers. (The table below shows some of the sodium compounds used in processed foods.) There has been a tendency over the last few years to increase the amount of sodium in these foods. Perhaps it is due to the fact that the food tasters employed by the food industry have a very high sodium intake and a suppressed salt taste threshold. If this were so, they would need very large amounts of sodium in the food they were tasting before a salty taste were to be appreciated. Another factor that may be important is that salty foods make you thirsty so you drink more which is, presumably, good for the drink industry.

The food manufacturers claim that if they reduce the amount of sodium, there may be wholesale rejection of some of their processed foods. There is no evidence for this but the manufacturers are unlikely to change unless there is considerable public pressure. However, in many countries in the West, food manufacturers are now producing a range of low-sodium products.

Sodium compounds used in processed foods

Compound	Purpose
Salt/sodium chloride	Flavour enhancer, preservative
Sodium bicarbonate	Used in self-raising flour*
Sodium nitrite	A preservative and also used to improve colouring in cured meats
Monosodium glutamate	Flavour enhancer
Sodium saccharin	A sweetener†
Sodium benzoate	Preservative in sauces, relishes and salad dressings
Sodium alginate	An emulsifier used in ice cream and drinks
Sodium sulphite	Preservative in some dried fruits

*Remember it is possible to use potassium bicarbonate, see page 35.
† The amount is usually trivial in terms of total sodium intake.

- Preservative: sodium chloride is the oldest preservative known, but its preservative role is nowadays very limited, with the introduction of other preservatives and particularly since the development of the refrigerator and deep-freeze.

- Part of the food processing: sodium is commonly used to form a gel with the meat and fat in canned meats. It acts as a binding agent, retaining water, so making the product heavier and, according to food manufacturers, more acceptable to the customer!
Sodium is also used to develop the full colour of products, particularly of ham, bacon and sausages.

- Labelling of foods with sodium content: more progressive food manufacturers in some countries are labelling their foods with the approximate sodium content. Usually,. this is the approximate sodium content per average serving. Some manufacturers are opposed to or are resisting· the labelling of the sodium content of foods. Yet, if foods were properly labelled with their sodium content, it would be possible for people who wished to stick to a low-sodium diet to buy a lot more processed food – anything with a sufficiently low-sodium content.

Other sources of sodium

Some medicines contain sodium and often pills are made up of sodium salts. However, the amount of sodium contained in these is usually very small.

One important source of sodium is some of the antacids.' Sodium bicarbonate has the highest content of all, but should not in any case be used as an antacid. Another is the various liver salts, or health or fruit salts. Indeed, any effervescent medicine is likely to contain sodium bicarbonate. To check which contain a lot of sodium, look at the bottles or ask your pharmacist.

Water and soft drinks   The sodium content of drinking water varies quite widely. In general it is not an important source of sodium as most people drink only one to two litres (two to four pints) of water a day. For example, the Thames water in London after treatment ranges from 6 mg of sodium per litre to 50 mg of sodium per litre, depending on the reservoir and source of water. In a few areas of the world the sodium content of water is much higher and can contribute to the total sodium intake in the diet, particularly if you are on a low-sodium diet. But in 99 per cent of cases there is no need to take drinking water into account.

Some mineral waters do contain very high amounts of sodium and you can certainly taste the salt; Vichy water contains approximately 70 mmol per litre (1600 mg per litre). Most others are low in sodium and can be safely drunk. The quantity is usually given on the label.

In soft drinks the sodium composition varies depending on the source of water that they are made with. On the whole, they are not an important source of sodium.

Water softeners   These are used to make soap lather more effectively. They work by adding sodium to the water to get rid of the hardening mineral, calcium. The amount of sodium added is not very large and drinking softened water will not increase sodium intake significantly. But there are other reasons for not drinking softened water. First, it is more likely to absorb metals from the pipes, particularly lead (though lead pipes are not common now), and second, there is evidence that the number of heart attacks in a community is directly related to the degree of softness of water – the harder the water, the fewer heart attacks. It is generally recommended that a tap with hard water should be left for drinking purposes if you have a water softener.

Salt substitutes

Low salt substitutes are usually a mixture of sodium and potassium, sometimes with the addition of a small amount of magnesium. People using substitutes say this is more acceptable than a pure potassium substitute as it does not have such a bitter aftertaste. But it still contains large amounts of sodium. A study done in Finland showed that people who used mineral salt consumed more of it than of sodium chloride as they thought the mineral salt was good for them, and so they did not after all reduce their sodium intake.

You will need to read the labels carefully. If a mineral salt contains sodium chloride, do not use it. Remember, if you have kidney disease never use a salt substitute without consulting your doctor.

Salt substitutes containing only potassium chloride and no sodium chloride have been around for many years and may be helpful for anyone who is in the habit of adding salt to food and finds it very difficult to give it up. However, our experience is that many people find these salt substitutes have a rather bitter aftertaste. If you want to try one, start with a very small amount added to the cooking or at the table. Make sure that it contains no sodium.

Potassium

Potassium is a vital constituent of our diet. It is present in the body mainly inside cells (see page 10). There is evidence in both animals and humans that not only a high-salt but also a low-potassium intake is likely to raise blood pressure. In addition there is evidence that increasing potassium intake does lower blood pressure, and it is interesting that vegetarians, who in general have a higher potassium intake than non-vegetarians, usually have lower blood pressure. An increase in potassium intake helps get rid of sodium through the kidney and it is probably this effect that lowers blood pressure.

Unlike sodium, potassium is present in large quantities in fruit and vegetables, meat and fish, and during evolution and in some primitive tribes today, large amounts of potassium were eaten – around 100 to 200 mmol (4 to 8 g) per day. As we eat less fruit and vegetables and more processed food in the West, potassium intake has fallen on average to around 30 to 80 mmols (1 to 3 g) per day. In northern Europe it is about half that of southern Europe, presumably as northern Europeans have been unused to eating fresh fruit and vegetables during the winter.

At the present time it would seem sensible to increase potassium intake, particularly by eating more fresh fruit and vegetables. Their taste, very lightly cooked or raw, is good without any added salt; the combination of onion, carrot and celery provides a superb flavour and is the base for many stocks and stews.

There is a possible danger in increasing potassium intake for people with kidney disease. The kidney may have problems in getting rid of high levels of potassium, which may lead to a rise in the level of potassium in the blood. If you have problems with the kidney, heart or liver, do not increase potassium intake or use a potassium salt substitute before consulting your doctor.

Other ways of eating healthily

Reducing your sodium intake is one of the most important factors in making the diet more healthy. If you are interested in eating a healthy diet it makes sense to combine the low-salt approach with other changes recommended by nutritional experts that will help control obesity, prevent the development of arterial disease and reduce the risk of heart disease.

Eat less fat   On average, people in Western countries need to reduce fat intake by one-third. Remember that fat is a very large source of calories and eating a high-fat diet is usually responsible for people being overweight. At the same time, saturated fat can raise your blood cholesterol.

To cut fat consumption, do not fry food but grill it. Cut all visible fat off meat; remember that even lean red meat contains large amounts of fat. Foods containing their own fat need nothing added for grilling; they can also be fried in a heavy non-stick pan without fat, and this way lose quite a lot of extra fat. Eat more fish and white meat.

Cut right down on milk, cheese, butter and margarine. If you try skimmed milk, remember that although it contains less fat than full milk, in large amounts it is a relatively high sodium-containing food.

As well as reducing total fat intake, polyunsaturated fats should be substituted for saturated fats. Use cooking oils that are labelled high in polyunsaturates, usually corn oil, soya bean oil and sunflower oil. Many cheaper blended vegetable oils are high in saturated fat. Monosaturated fats, such as olive oil may be the best to use.

Eat less sugar   Sugar is second to fat as a source of calories. Too many calories mean that you will get fat. Try to cut back on sweets, chocolates and soft drinks. A high sugar intake also increases the chances of diabetes developing and is the prime cause of tooth decay. Most people need to reduce the amount of sugar they eat by a half.

Eat more fibre   Fibre is the name given to a range of complex plant substances that pass through the intestine and are not absorbed. By providing roughage, they aid digestion and help prevent constipation. There is some evidence that they may reduce blood cholesterol and blood sugar as well as a suggestion that they may even lower blood pressure. Fibre is mainly present in wholemeal flour, oats and other cereals, in fresh vegetables and fruit.

Fruit and vegetables   Try to eat more fresh fruit and vegetables. This means that you will be eating less fat, more fibre and potassium, at the same time as eating very little sodium. If you can't always buy fresh, the best substitute is frozen, not dried or canned, which has less nutritional value and often salt added in the latter.

HOW TO COOK WITHOUT SALT

Here are some guidelines on cooking for a low-salt diet. Cutting out salt and salty foods and substituting new flavours soon becomes second nature, and introduces variety into your eating. The table on page 32 outlines the broad groups of foods with high and low-salt content.

1. *Do not use any form of cooking or table salt*, or other forms of salt such as sea salt, garlic salt, celery salt. Remember that flavour enhancers nearly always contain sodium, particularly in the form of monosodium glutamate. Do not use low salt substitutes, which contain a mixture of potassium and sodium salts and are not suitable for a restricted sodium diet. However, you may use a pure potassium salt substitute. Make sure that it is one that does not contain sodium and use it very sparingly as you may find that it has a bitter aftertaste, particularly when you first use it.

2. *Replace salt by various spices*, such as freshly ground pepper, paprika pepper, cayenne pepper, chilli powder (use this sparingly at first; you may find its flavour very powerful), ginger, fresh or ground, cinnamon, curry powder, garam masala, nutmeg and clove.

3. *Make your own low-salt stock*. It can be stored and will always come in useful (page 45).

4. For varied flavours try mustard powder, lemon juice, vinegar, white or red wine, cider or beer.

5. Use plenty of onions, shallots, garlic, fresh chillis (use with care as some are very hot). All of these are particularly good added to stews.

6. Fresh herbs, such as parsley, chives, mint, thyme, sage, rosemary, basil and tarragon are all excellent to flavour a salt-free dish. They can be grown in pots on a sunny windowsill, and can be bought from any good garden centre or grown from seeds. Fresh herbs can be frozen or dried.

7. If fresh herbs are not available, they can be replaced by dried herbs. Mixed dried herbs are excellent and easy to use.

   Most of the recipes use dried herbs for convenience, but try using fresh herbs if you have some and adjust the quantity according to your taste. In general, you will need slightly more of the fresh herbs than the equivalent dried.

Vegetables
- Eat as much fresh vegetables and salads as you like.

Guide to sodium content

Foods with a low-sodium content (eat freely)
Vegetables: all kinds except tinned or dried
Fruit: all kinds, fresh, frozen, dried or tinned
Meat, fish, eggs, poultry (not commercially prepared)
Salt-free butter, salt-free margarine, fresh cream
Salt-free bread, pasta and rice
Unsalted nuts
Fruit juices, squashes and cordials
Tea, coffee
Sugar, jam, marmalade, honey, boiled sweets, peppermints

Foods with a medium-sodium content (limit or avoid)
Tinned vegetables
Milk, yoghurt and milk puddings
Salted butter and margarine
Bought bread, cakes, biscuits, pastry
Breakfast cereals
Bottled sauces and ketchups
Chocolate

Foods with a high-sodium content (do not eat)
Table salt
Bacon, ham, cured meat, tinned meat, salami, sausages, bought pate
Smoked fish, tinned fish
Cheese
Tinned and packet soups
Stock cubes, yeast and meat extracts
Vegetable juices, soy sauce

For more detailed information on the sodium content of various foods see pages 98–106.

● Frozen vegetables can usually be eaten as most have no sodium added (check the label). Remember though that prepared vegetables with a sauce have had sodium added.

● When cleaning vegetables never use salt or sodium bi-carbonate.

● Do not add any salt to the cooking.

● It is a good idea to try to retain the potassium when cooking vegetables. Do not boil but steam them. Put the vegetables in an ordinary pan, add a small quantity of unsalted water, approximately 100 ml/3.5 fl oz per 450 g/1 lb of vegetable. Cover the pan and cook over very low heat until just tender and still crisp. Alternatively, you can cook vegetables over a pan of simmering water in a colander. It is not really necessary to have a special steaming pan, the flavour is still retained. Alternatively use a microwave.

• If a sauce is required for the vegetables, for example, cauliflower or spinach, or gravy for meat, use the normal amount of boiling water and retain the liquid left from the cooking, which is salt-free, has a good flavour and is rich in potassium.

If you are not using the cooking liquid this way, keep it and use it later as stock either for soup or a stew.

• Avoid any canned or dried vegetables except canned tomatoes, which do not usually contain any salt (check the label on the tin) and cans labelled 'no salt added'. Do not use instant potato or tomato juice. Salt-free tomato puree can be obtained; look at the label. If you are not able to find one, use a small amount of the ordinary type. This will not contribute too much salt to your intake.

• Pulses (dried beans, peas and lentils) are low in sodium and fat, high in fibre and make a good and economical substitute for meat as they contain protein. Soaking and cooking times depend on the type, and the packet will give instructions. Always soak and cook pulses in salt-free water. It is very important that they are boiled for at least 10 minutes at the beginning of the cooking time as some beans can cause acute vomiting and diarrhoea if not boiled.

Fruit
• You can eat any kind of fruit: fresh, frozen, canned or dried. If you eat canned fruit try to choose those in their natural juice without large amounts of added sugar. Remember that if you eat the skin of the fruit you will also be eating more fibre.

Meat and poultry
• You can eat any kind of lean beef, pork, lamb, rabbit, liver, kidney or poultry, whether fresh or frozen. Remember, however, that frozen prepared meat dishes will have salt added.

Do not eat any kind of commercially prepared meat products such as sausages, canned meat, beefburgers, pate, pies or meat spreads. You can make your own beefburgers and pate free of added salt (see pages 50, 72).

• When cooking any meat or poultry, never add salt. Flavour it instead with fresh or dried herbs such as rosemary or mint for lamb, thyme or sage for pork, black pepper and mixed herbs for beef, tarragon, sage or thyme for chicken – or any other herbs you may like to try. You can also rub the skin of the meat with mustard powder, but remember that prepared mustards have salt added so do not use these. If you like the flavour of garlic, try making small cuts in a joint and filling them with garlic slivers before roasting.

• Avoid frying meat. Grill or cook in the oven whenever you can. If you do fry it, use the minimum of oil and a non-stick pan. A lot of meat can even be fried without any added fat, as sufficient will be released during cooking.

● You must try to avoid any kind of smoked meat, for instance, bacon and ham, as these have had large amounts of sodium chloride and other sodium salts added to them. If, occasionally, you wish to eat a slice of bacon, or to cook a ham, you can reduce the salt content by soaking the meat in water for at least a day or, in the case of sliced bacon, for a few hours. Change the water two or three times during soaking then drain the meat and wash it under a cold tap. If you are cooking a ham, you can boil it for half the cooking time and change the water once during cooking. Finish cooking the ham by baking it in the oven. Even with all this preparation, ham will still contain large amounts of salt so do not eat too much – try to avoid it if you can!

Fish
● You can eat as much fresh or frozen fish as you like. It may be baked or grilled. If you fry fish, use the minimum of oil.

● You must try to avoid smoked fish and all commercially prepared fish such as fish fingers, fish cakes, tinned fish and frozen fish that is prepared in sauce and breadcrumbs. All of these have had salt added to them.

Shellfish
● Shellfish are relatively high in sodium content. However, small amounts are not absolutely forbidden! Remember that you can reduce the sodium content by boiling them in salt-free water.
Commercially prepared prawns often have a glaze added to them which has sodium in it.

Dairy foods
● Unsalted butter is available in many supermarkets, but it is preferable to use salt-free polyunsaturated margarine which can be bought in most health food shops.
It is much better to grill food, but if you must fry it, use polyunsaturated vegetable oils such as corn, sunflower, safflower or soya bean, or best of all, olive oil.

● All cheese contains salt. If you must include it in your cooking, use it very sparingly and choose a cheese with a low-sodium content, such as mild cheddar, parmesan, cottage cheese or mozzarella cheese. Grating the cheese makes it go further in many dishes.
Cream cheese is quite low in sodium, but use it only occasionally as it has a very high fat content.

● Low-fat yoghurt may be used in small quantities.

● Fresh cream, whilst high in saturated fats and not recommended for that reason, is low in sodium and may be eaten on special occasions.

● Milk contains saturated fat and relatively large quantities of sodium so use only small amounts. Skimmed milk has the same sodium content as whole milk but contains less fat and is preferable.

● Eggs may be eaten as a main meal instead of meat or fish, but don't forget that the yolks are high in cholesterol, so use whole eggs sparingly.

Bread, cakes and cereals

● Try to cook with plain wholemeal flour. Plain white flour can be used in some recipes or mixed with wholemeal flour. Do not use self-raising flour, ordinary baking powder or bicarbonate of soda, as they all contain sodium. You can buy baking powder substitute which is salt-free and contains potassium. This is available from some health food shops, or you can ask your local chemist to make it up (see page 96). You can make your own self-raising flour by mixing plain flour with the potassium baking powder substitute.

● Bread that you buy in the shops is a high-salt food. Some health food shops have salt-free bread but it is generally hard to find. You may be able to persuade your local baker to cook a batch of salt-free bread for you, and you can then freeze it. Why not instead try making your own salt-free wholemeal or white bread using the recipes in this book.

● Remember that all manufactured biscuits, cakes and crispbreads contain salt or sodium and are often high in saturated fat so make your own using the recipes in this book. If your favourite cake or biscuit recipe is not amongst them, use your recipe but replace the ordinary margarine or butter by polyunsaturated salt-free margarine and the self-raising flour by plain flour and a baking powder substitute.

All cakes and biscuits contain fairly large amounts of fat so try to keep them for special occasions only.

● Most breakfast cereals contain quite large amounts of salt; you must avoid these. Those that are low in sodium are Puffed Wheat, Shredded Wheat, Sugar Puffs and porridge oats.

● You can eat any kind of pasta, preferably wholemeal, or rice, again preferably brown unpolished or wild rice. Remember to cook these in unsalted water.

● Other cereals such as wheat, oats, rye, barley, maize and buckwheat are all salt-free and can be used.

Sauces

● Do not use any manufactured sauces, for example, tomato ketchup, salad cream, Worcestershire sauce, soya sauce, mayonnaise, horseradish or prepared mustards unless labelled salt-free. Some health food shops stock a range of sauces which are low in sodium, and you can make your own salt-free tomato sauce or mayonnaise using our recipes.

● Do not use stock cubes, gravy powders and concentrated vegetable, yeast or meat extracts as they are all very high in sodium. Make your own low-salt stock using the recipes in the book.

Drinks
● Tea, coffee, most fizzy drinks such as lemonade and colas, fruit juices, squashes and cordials are low in sodium. Soda water, one or two mineral waters, and some other drinks such as Lucozade, have some sodium in them (see page 27).

● Alcoholic beverages can be taken in moderation: 1–2 glasses of wine or ½ l/1 pint of beer or 1 or 2 measures of spirits per day maximum (the sodium contents of the different alcoholic beverages are listed on page 106 but are generally quite low.) Remember that excessive alcohol intake causes damage to the liver and other vital organs. It is also associated with high blood pressure.

● Milk and skimmed milk are high in sodium (see above) and should be used only sparingly as an additive to tea or coffee.

Packed lunches
● These represent quite a problem as the conventional sandwich lunch has a high-sodium content. Reduce this by making sandwiches with salt-free, preferably wholemeal bread (see recipe page 94) and use polyunsaturated salt-free margarine or unsalted butter.

● Fill the sandwiches with a selection of lettuce, cucumber, tomato, celery, carrot, watercress and onion combined with homemade salt-free mayonnaise or dressing;

or

salt-free pâté (see page 50) or your own cold, cooked meat, for example, beef, pork, lamb, chicken or turkey – do not use ham, sausage or salami, tinned meat, commercially prepared pâté or meat spreads;

or

you can occasionally use eggs, a little cottage or cream cheese, or a small slice of mild cheddar cheese but remember the warnings about fat and cholesterol in dairy products;

or

try sweet fillings such as mashed banana, chopped dates or a little cream cheese mixed with nuts and raisins or chopped pineapple.

● You could sometimes include a homemade salt-free quiche or pasty filled with meat or vegetables. 'Sausage' rolls can be made salt-free with a spiced minced meat mixture instead of the sausage. Any pastry has a high-fat content so these should be taken only occasionally, for variety.

● You can eat any fresh salad with your own salt-free dressing, but do not buy commercially prepared, takeaway salads.

● Fresh fruit is a perfect ending to any meal. Always try to include it. Mixed salt-free nuts and raisins, homemade cakes, biscuits or fruit pie are alternatives, but try to keep the baked foods for special occasions as they are high in fat and calories.

Availability of low-sodium or salt-free products

With the increasing publicity about the dangers of salt, many food manufacturers are now producing low-sodium or no-salt-added products. Some are obtainable in supermarkets and others are available only through health food shops. Many of these products are suitable for people on a low-salt diet, but you will need to read the labels very carefully. They cannot be listed individually due to wide variations from one country to another and the fact that they are coming out in increasing numbers every few months. They can be broadly categorized into:

1. **Dairy products** eg, low-sodium butter, low-sodium margarine (preferably labelled 'high in polyunsaturates') and in some countries, low-sodium cheeses.
2. **Cereal products** eg, low-sodium bread and biscuits. It is important to ask how much sodium is in bread; try to obtain bread with none added.
3. **Canned products**, either low-sodium or no-salt-added eg, vegetables, soups, meats.
4. **Low-sodium sauces** eg, tomato ketchup, mayonnaise, mustard.
5. **Low-sodium dried products**, eg, dried soups.

It is likely that there will be an increasing range of all these products, including frozen prepared meals. The greater the demand, the greater will be the availability of these products.

Don't forget the three steps in the low-salt diet:

1. Remember that initally the food will taste bland.
2. Allow time for your taste receptors to adjust, probably around two weeks.

3. You will then find you will be able to detect sodium in food very easily. Your new diet will taste much better and you will be able to distinguish between different foods very much more easily.

THE RECIPES

Weights and measures

The sodium and potassium content per serving for each recipe are shown in millimoles (mmol) and milligrams (mg). For simplicity, in the table on pages 98–106, giving both the sodium and potassium content of individual foods, they are only given in mmol. If you want to convert the mmol figure to mg, multiply by 23 for sodium and 39 for potassium. If you wish to convert mg into grams of sodium, divide by 1000. If you want to convert the sodium content of a meal in grams to its equivalent in sodium chloride (salt), you should multiply by 2.5.

In the recipes and tables the figures have been rounded up or down to the nearest whole number. Figures coming out at less than 1 mmol are considered negligible and listed Tr (trace) in the table.

One level teaspoon of salt contains 120 mmol of sodium and one level tablespoon of salt contains 360 mmol of sodium. The average sodium intake in the West is approximately between 120–250 mmol per day. If you stick to the diet outlined in this book, you will reduce your sodium intake to around 20–80 mmol per day, depending on how strictly you keep away from processed foods. It is very important to remember that whilst sodium chloride (salt) is added to the food during cooking, or at the table and sometimes as a preservative and is the main source of sodium in our diets, we must also take into account other forms of sodium which are added: sodium bicarbonate, monosodium glutamate, as well as the sodium naturally occurring in foods.

All figures for calculation of the recipes and tables have been taken from McCance and Widdowson's *Composition of Foods* (HMSO) unless otherwise stated. If further details are required, this is a good book to consult.

The energy value is given in kilocalories. Kilocalories are commonly known as calories.

The recipe ingredients are in both metric and Imperial measurements. Slight roundings up have been made, so do not mix the two in any one recipe.

The spoon measurements used in the recipes throughout are level unless otherwise stated. One teaspoon (tsp) = 5 ml; 1 tablespoon (tbsp) = 15 ml. To ensure success, check the size of the spoons you are using.

Australian users should remember that as their tablespoon has been converted to 20 ml, and is therefore larger than the tablespoon measurement used in the recipes in this book, they should use 3 × 5 ml tsp where instructed to use 1 × 15 ml tbsp.

Sample meal plan

If you follow this meal plan, using recipes in the book as well as salt-free fresh foods, you will have a well balanced, healthy diet.

Choose one of the suggested dishes from each of the categories in the different meals, and ring the changes often enough to provide interest in your diet.

Regulate your calorie intake according to your needs by checking the calorie values of the recipes and in the tables on pages 98–106.

Don't forget, all food must be cooked and prepared without salt.

Breakfast
Fruit juice (not tomato)
Grapefruit, fresh or tinned
Prunes, stewed fruit

Unsalted cereal: Shredded Wheat, Puffed Wheat, Sugar Puffs or
porridge with a small amount of milk
Boiled, poached, scrambled egg occasionally

Salt-free bread, unsalted butter or salt-free margarine
Jam, marmalade or honey

Tea or coffee

NB If ordinary bread, rolls or crackers are taken, refer to the table (page 101) and count them in your daily salt allowance.

Lunch or light meal
Salt-free bread or rolls filled with cold sliced plain roast meats,
egg, homemade meat loaf or pâté (page 50), or salad
Homemade savoury pastries or quiche (page 92) filled with
unsalted minced meat or vegetables
Salt-free crackers and a little cream cheese, cucumber and
tomato
Homemade beefburgers in a salt-free roll (pages 72, 95) with
salad
Eggs, scrambled, poached, boiled (or occasionally fried) with
baked or grilled tomatoes

Mixed salad with salt-free meat, eggs, cooked unsalted beans or unsalted peanuts

Rice salad (page 57) with a selection of chopped vegetables, nuts

Fresh fruit, mixed salt-free nuts and raisins, homemade cake or biscuit (pages 84–91) (made with salt-free baking powder)

Tea, coffee, squash, fruit juices

Dinner or main meal
Homemade soup without stock cubes (pages 45–7)
Homemade pâté with salt-free bread (pages 50, 94)
Grapefruit, fruit juice (not tomato)
Avocado pear with vinaigrette dressing or homemade mayonnaise (page 48)

Meat or fish, grilled, baked or roast
Meat or vegetable casserole (pages 60, 74)
Homemade pie or pasty (page 80)
Nut or bean dish (page 59)

Vegetable or salad (use salt-free dressing)

Rice, pasta, potatoes or bread

Fresh or tinned fruit
Jelly or small ice cream
Water ice (page 81)
Fruit pie or flan (pages 81–2)
Steamed or baked sponge made with salt-free baking powder
Baked apple

Double cream or small quantity of custard sauce

Tea, coffee

NB If wine, beer or other alcoholic beverage is taken, check the amount of sodium it contains in the table (page 106).

A salt-free meal: Avocado with mayonnaise (*bottom*, see page 48), Chicken with rice and velouté sauce (*centre left*, see page 79), Tossed green salad with curry dressing (*centre right*, see page 56), French plum flan (*top*, see page 82)
OVERLEAF: Fish coquille (*left*, see page 51), Celery, apple and walnut salad (*bottom right*, see page 58), Country pâté (*top right*, see page 50).

SOUPS

STOCKS

When making soups do not use stock cubes as they all contain salt. Instead make your own stock. The method is simple: place in a large pan any bones and roughly chopped vegetables, especially carrots, onions and celery. Add 1 to 1½ 1/2 to 3 pints of water, flavour with your favourite herbs, one bay leaf and a few peppercorns, bring to the boil, reduce the heat and cover. Simmer for about 2 hours, then strain and allow to cool. Stock can be kept, covered, for about one week in a refrigerator or it can be frozen and used when required.

If you prefer to use a pure vegetable stock, omit the bones and add a few extra vegetables, such as leeks or turnips.

In all the soup recipes, water can be used instead of stock, but the flavour of the soup will, of course, not be as good as a soup made with homemade stock.

Garlic and tomato soup

Serves 4
Each serving: negligible sodium; 10 mmol (407 mg) potassium; 65 Kcal

15 ml/1 tbsp vegetable oil
450 g/1 lb tomatoes, chopped
2 onions, chopped
4 cloves garlic, finely chopped
5 ml/1 tsp dried thyme

1 bay leaf
25 g/1 oz plain flour
pinch chilli powder
freshly ground pepper

Heat the oil in a pan. Add the tomatoes, onions, garlic, thyme and bay leaf and cook slowly for about 10 minutes, stirring occasionally. Stir in the flour. Pour in 1 1/1¾ pints water, bring to the boil, reduce the heat, add the pepper and chilli powder, cover and simmer for 30 minutes. Remove the bay leaf and reduce the soup to a purée in an electric blender or by rubbing through a sieve.

Return to the pan, reheat and serve hot.

Garlic and tomato soup *(top)*, Split pea soup *(bottom*, see page 47)

Country vegetable soup

Serves 4
Each serving: 2 mmol (44 mg) sodium; 21 mmol (809 mg) potassium; 162 Kcal

15 ml/1 tbsp vegetable oil
2 medium-sized potatoes, peeled and chopped
2 leeks, sliced
l large onion, chopped
2 carrots, diced
2 celery leaves (optional)

50 g/2 oz split peas (optional)
25 g/1 oz plain flour
1 l/1¾ pints homemade salt-free stock or water (do not use stock cubes)
freshly ground pepper
pinch chilli powder

Heat the oil in a large pan. Add the vegetables and cook over moderate heat for 5–10 minutes, without browning them. Stir in the flour. Pour in the stock or water, bring to the boil, reduce the heat, season with pepper and chilli powder, cover and simmer for about 20 minutes, until vegetables are tender.

If desired, reduce to a purée in an electric blender or by rubbing through a sieve.

Return to the pan, reheat and serve hot.

Fish soup

Serves 4
Each serving: 3 mmol (77 mg) sodium; 12 mmol (492 mg) potassium; 113 Kcal

3 cloves
2 whole onions
225 g/8 oz white fish, boned, skinned and chopped
2 carrots, diced
1 small leek, chopped
3 cloves garlic, finely chopped

150 ml/¼ pint white wine (optional)
5 ml/1 tsp dried mixed herbs
5 ml/1 tsp fennel seeds (optional)
1 egg yolk
15 ml/1 tbsp lemon juice
pinch grated nutmeg
freshly ground pepper

Stick the cloves into the onions. Put the fish in a large pan and add the onions, carrots, leek and garlic. Pour in 1 l/1¾ pints water and wine. Season with pepper, mixed herbs and fennel. Bring to the boil, reduce the heat, cover and simmer for 30 minutes. Reduce to a purée in an electric blender or by rubbing through a sieve. Return to the pan. Mix together the egg yolk, lemon juice, nutmeg and pepper and stir into the soup. Reheat gently without boiling, stirring constantly.

Serve hot.

Curried vegetable soup

Serves 4

Each serving: negligible sodium; 12.3 mmol (479 mg) potassium; 61 Kcal

15 ml/1 tbsp vegetable oil
1 onion, sliced
2 cloves garlic, finely chopped
225 g/8 oz French beans, chopped
3 tomatoes, skinned and chopped

1 potato, chopped
5 ml/1 tsp curry powder (or more to taste)
freshly ground pepper

Heat the oil in a pan. Add the onion and garlic and cook gently. Stir in the beans, tomatoes, potato, curry powder and pepper. Pour in 1 1/1¾ pints water, bring to the boil, reduce the heat, cover and simmer for 35–40 minutes. Reduce to a purée in an electric blender or by rubbing through a sieve.

Return to the pan and add more pepper or curry powder if necessary. Reheat and serve hot.

Split pea soup See photograph, page 44

Serves 4

Each serving: 2 mmol (36 mg) sodium; 16 mmol (625 mg) potassium; 170 Kcal

225 g/8 oz split peas
1 carrot, diced
1 onion, finely chopped
2 sprigs parsley

1 small bay leaf
5 ml/1 tsp dried thyme
freshly ground pepper

Soak the split peas for one hour in cold water. Drain the peas, place in a saucepan, add 1.3 l/2¼ pints water and bring to the boil. Reduce the heat, skim off the scum, add the carrot, onion, parsley, bay leaf and thyme. Season with pepper, cover and cook for about 1½ hours. Reduce to a purée in an electric blender or by rubbing through a sieve.

Return to the pan, reheat and serve hot, garnished with bread croûtons fried in a little vegetable oil and chopped parsley or sorrel.

SAUCES, SNACKS AND STARTERS

Tomato sauce

Serves 4
Each serving: negligible sodium; 17 mmol (680 mg) potassium; 36 Kcal

*900 g/2 lb ripe tomatoes, skinned
   and chopped
1 medium size onion, finely chopped
3 cloves garlic, finely chopped
1 bay leaf*

*10 ml/2 tsp dried mixed herbs or
   15 ml/1 tbsp chopped mixed fresh
   herbs
freshly ground pepper*

Plunge the tomatoes in boiling water for a few seconds, then skin them. Put the chopped onion, garlic and tomato in a pan. Add the bay leaf and herbs, season with pepper and simmer, uncovered, for about 1 hour. If the sauce becomes too dry, add a little water. Remove the bay leaf and serve hot.

   If liked, the sauce can be reduced to a purée in an electric blender or by rubbing it through a sieve.

Alternatives   For a spicy tomato sauce add ½ tsp chilli powder.
   If fresh tomatoes are unavailable, salt-free canned tomatoes can be used instead.

Mayonnaise

Serves 4–6
Each serving: negligible sodium; negligible potassium; 467–700 Kcal
Each level tablespoon (15 ml): negligible sodium; negligible potassium; 140 Kcal

*2 egg yolks
300 ml/½ pint unsaturated vegetable
   oil
15 ml/1 tbsp white wine vinegar*

freshly ground pepper

*Garnish:
chopped chives or parsley*

Place the egg yolks in a bowl and beat well. At first add the oil drop by drop, whisking continuously until the mayonnaise starts to thicken, then add the remaining oil in a slow stream, whisking all the time. Stir in the vinegar and pepper and garnish with chopped chives or parsley.

Crudités with garlic mayonnaise dip

Serves 6
Each serving: 4 mmol (105 mg) sodium; 17 mmol (654 mg) potassium; 116 Kcal

Garlic mayonnaise:
4 cloves garlic, crushed
2 egg yolks
300 ml/½ pint olive oil
15 ml/1 tbsp wine vinegar
freshly ground pepper

4 carrots, cut into matchsticks
½ cauliflower, cut into florets
1 green pepper, cut into strips
1 red pepper, cut into strips
4 celery sticks, cut into equal lengths
12 spring onions, trimmed

Crudités:
4 tomatoes, sliced or quartered
½ cucumber, cut into strips

Garnish:
chopped chives or chopped parsley

To make the garlic mayonnaise, mix together the crushed garlic and the egg yolks. Beat well. Add the oil, drop by drop, whisking all the time. Stir in the vinegar and pepper.

Arrange the vegetables on a serving dish. Sprinkle the chopped chives or parsley over the garlic mayonnaise and hand separately.

Roasted peanuts

Each level tablespoon: negligible sodium; 2 mmol (82 mg) potassium; 71 Kcal

Use plain unsalted peanuts which can be obtained from health shops and some greengrocers.

Heat the oven to 180°C/350°F/gas 4.

Place the peanuts on a baking tray and bake for about 15 minutes, shaking the tray occasionally. After baking, the skin of the peanuts will come away easily. Eat cold.

Alternatives   Hazelnuts and almonds can be roasted in the same way.

Hummus

Serves 2–3
Each serving: negligible sodium; 7–10 mmol (271–407 mg) potassium; 152–228 Kcal

100 g/4 oz chick peas
4 cloves garlic, crushed
2.5 ml/½ tsp chilli powder
freshly ground pepper
15 ml/1 tbsp olive oil

15 ml/1 tbsp wine vinegar

Garnish:
chopped parsley
paprika pepper

Soak the chick peas overnight in cold water. Drain, then cook them in plenty of unsalted water for 2–3 hours, or until tender. Drain, keeping about 200 ml/7 fl oz of the cooking liquid. Blend or mash the chick peas and the water until smooth and stir in the garlic, chilli powder and pepper. Add the olive oil and vinegar, little by little, stirring all the time. The mixture should be smooth and fairly firm. Garnish with chopped parsley and paprika pepper.

Serve with sliced raw vegetables and salt-free wholemeal or pitta bread (pages 94, 95).

An alternative   This can be varied by adding 15 ml/1 tbsp salt-free tahini (sesame seed paste) with the oil, lemon juice and parsley.

Leeks vinaigrette

Serves 4
Each serving: negligible sodium; 10 mmol (386 mg) potassium; 69 Kcal

450 g/1 lb young leeks, trimmed and halved	*1 small onion, finely chopped*
	1 clove garlic, crushed
	freshly ground pepper
Dressing:	
45 ml/3 tbsp olive oil	Garnish:
15 ml/1 tbsp wine vinegar	*chopped parsley*

Put the leeks in a pan, add 100 ml/3.5 fl oz water, cover and cook over low heat for about 15 minutes. Drain the leeks and cool.

To make the vinaigrette, mix together the oil and vinegar, add the onion and garlic, and season with pepper.

Arrange the leeks on a serving dish, pour the vinaigrette over and garnish with chopped parsley.

Country pâté   See photograph, page 43

Serves 6 to 8
Each serving: 4–5 mmol (89–119 mg) sodium; 6–8 mmol (386–580 mg) potassium; 298–397 Kcal

450 g/1 lb fresh pork	*10 ml/2 tsp dried mixed herbs*
350 g/12 oz pork livers, minced	*pinch cayenne pepper*
1 onion, finely chopped	*15 ml/1 tbsp brandy*
2 cloves garlic, crushed	*freshly ground pepper*
1 egg, beaten	

Heat the oven to 160°C/325°F/gas 3.

Mix together the minced pork, livers, onion, garlic, beaten egg, mixed herbs, cayenne, pepper and brandy. Season with pepper.

Turn into a terrine or loaf tin and cover with foil. Bake for about 2 hours.

Cool in the tin before turning out.

Fish coquille
See photograph, page 42

Serves 4

Each serving: 6 mmol (131 mg) sodium; 7 mmol (262 mg) potassium; 146 Kcal

45 ml/3 tbsp skimmed milk	*freshly ground pepper*
2 egg yolks	*1 clove garlic, crushed*
50 g/2 oz low-salt cheese (mild cheddar, gouda, edam), grated	*225 g/8 oz cooked white fish, eg, cod or haddock, skinned and flaked*
15 ml/1 tbsp lemon juice	*50 g/2 oz salt-free wholemeal bread-crumbs – optional (see page 96)*
15 ml/1 tbsp chopped parsley	

Heat the oven to 190°C/375°F/gas 5.

Mix together the milk, egg yolks, half the cheese, lemon juice and chopped parsley. Season with pepper and crushed garlic. Stir in the fish. Turn the mixture into 4 scallop shells or individual baking dishes and stand on a baking sheet. Sprinkle with the remaining cheese and the breadcrumbs, if using, and bake for 10–15 minutes, until golden brown.

Mexican-style egg
See photograph, page 53

Serves 2

Each serving: 6 mmol (148 mg) sodium; 14 mmol (527 mg) potassium; 162 Kcal

15 ml/1 tbsp unsaturated vegetable oil	*1 green pepper, sliced*
1 onion, finely chopped	*2.5 ml/½ tsp chilli powder*
3 tomatoes, sliced	*freshly ground pepper*
	3 eggs, beaten

Heat the oil in a pan, add the onion, tomatoes and green pepper and cook over moderate heat for 5 minutes. Add the chilli powder and season with pepper. Stir in the beaten eggs and cook them over low heat for a few minutes, stirring continuously. Serve immediately.

Spaghetti with ground basil sauce
See photograph, page 53

Serves 4

Each serving: negligible sodium; 13 mmol (493 mg) potassium; 470 Kcal

450 g/1 lb wholemeal spaghetti
45 ml/3 tbsp finely chopped fresh
  basil leaves
45 ml/3 tbsp finely chopped fresh
  parsley

2 cloves garlic, crushed
45 ml/3 tbsp olive oil
freshly ground pepper

Cook the spaghetti in plenty of unsalted boiling water for about 12–15 minutes, until just tender.

Meanwhile, prepare the basil sauce. Combine the basil, parsley and garlic and pound to a paste. Stir in the olive oil and pepper. Drain the spaghetti and return it to the pan. Stir in the basil sauce. Mix thoroughly and serve immediately.

Pizza

Serves 2–4
Each serving: 2–5 mmol (58–116 mg) sodium; 13–25 mmol (489–978 mg) potassium; 206–412 Kcal
Using tinned tomatoes, each serving: 4–8 mmol (87–114 mg) sodium; 12–24 mmol (466–932 mg) potassium; 204–408 Kcal

Bread dough:
2.5 ml/½ tsp dried yeast
100 g/4 oz plain strong wholemeal
  flour

Filling:
75 g/3 oz mozzarella cheese

450 g/1 lb tomatoes, sliced
or
1 tin chopped tomatoes
1 onion, finely chopped
10 ml/2 tsp dried mixed herbs
15 ml/1 tbsp olive oil
freshly ground pepper

To make the bread dough, pour approximately 100 ml/3.5 fl oz warm water into a small bowl and sprinkle on the yeast. Stir. Set aside in a warm place for 10–15 minutes, until frothy. Place the flour in a bowl, make a well in the centre and pour in the yeast liquid. Mix to a firm dough, turn on to a lightly floured surface and knead until smooth. Leave covered in a warm place until doubled in size.

Heat the oven to 230°C/450°F/gas 8.

Grease a 28 cm/11 in pizza tray. Roll out the dough and place on the pizza tray. Cut the cheese into small pieces and arrange on the dough. Add the sliced tomatoes or tinned chopped tomatoes, onion, garlic, herbs and olive oil. Season with pepper. Bake for 15–20 minutes, then serve straight away.

Spaghetti with ground basil sauce (*top*, see page 51), Mexican-style egg (*centre*, see page 51), Pizza (bottom)

Cracked wheat salad

Serves 4
Each serving: negligible sodium; 10 mmol (377 mg) potassium; 240 Kcal

225 g/8 oz cracked wheat
2 small onions, finely chopped
2 tomatoes, finely chopped
30 ml/2 tbsp olive oil
15 ml/1 tbsp lemon juice
30 ml/2 tbsp chopped parsley

freshly ground pepper

Garnish:
lettuce leaves
slices of tomato

Cover the cracked wheat with cold water and soak for 30 minutes. Drain and squeeze out as much water as possible, then spread out on a cloth to dry. Mix together the cracked wheat with the onions and tomatoes. Add the olive oil, lemon juice and chopped parsley. Season with pepper. If too dry, add a little water to moisten it.

Line a large serving dish with lettuce leaves and arrange the cracked wheat on top. Decorate with some tomato slices. Extra lettuce leaves are served separately to scoop out the salad.

SALADS

Greek cucumber salad

Serves 4
Each serving: 2 mmol (34 mg) sodium; 4 mmol (134 mg) potassium; 27 Kcal

30 ml/2 tbsp low-fat plain yoghurt
15 ml/1 tbsp cottage cheese, sieved
15 ml/1 tbsp wine vinegar
15 ml/1 tbsp olive oil
2 cloves garlic, crushed

freshly ground pepper
1 cucumber, thinly sliced

Garnish:
chopped parsley or chives

Mix together the yoghurt, cottage cheese, vinegar, oil and garlic. Season with pepper. Toss the sliced cucumber in the dressing and garnish with chopped parsley or chives.

Cracked wheat salad (*top*), Greek cucumber salad (*centre*), Lentil salad with garlic croûtons (*bottom*, see page 57)

Summer salad

Serves 4
**Each serving: negligible sodium; 16 mmol (562 mg) potassium;
171 Kcal**

Dressing:
45 ml/3 tbsp olive oil
15 ml/1 tbsp lemon juice
5 ml/1 tsp oregano
freshly ground pepper

Salad:
1 small cucumber, sliced
4 tomatoes, quartered

1 green pepper, sliced
1 small onion, finely chopped
50 g/2 oz button mushrooms, sliced
1 small avocado pear, sliced

Garnish:
chopped chives or
  chopped spring onions

Mix together the dressing ingredients. Add the salad ingredients,
toss well and garnish with chopped chives or chopped spring
onions.

Tomato salad

Serves 4
**Each serving: negligible sodium; 10 mmol (376 mg) potassium;
44 Kcal**

6 large tomatoes, sliced
1 small onion, finely chopped

Dressing:
1 clove garlic, crushed

5 ml/1 tsp chopped basil
5 ml/1 tsp chopped tarragon
30 ml/2 tbsp olive oil
freshly ground pepper

Place the sliced tomatoes in a serving dish. Arrange the chopped
onion on top. Stir the crushed garlic and herbs into the olive oil.
Season with pepper. Pour the dressing over the tomatoes and
serve.

Tossed green salad with curry dressing

Serves 4
**Each serving: negligible sodium; 2 mmol (89 mg) potassium;
28 Kcal**

pinch dry mustard
pinch demerara sugar
15 ml/1 tbsp wine or cider vinegar
*30 ml/2 tbsp unsaturated vegetable
  oil*

1 clove garlic, crushed
5 ml/1 tsp curry powder
freshly ground pepper
1 green lettuce, separated into leaves

Mix together the mustard, sugar and vinegar. Add the oil, garlic
and curry powder. Season with pepper. Just before serving, toss
the lettuce leaves in the dressing.

Lentil salad with garlic croûtons

Serves 4 See photograph, page 54
Each serving: 1 mmol (30 mg) sodium; 16 mmol (633 mg) potassium; 278 Kcal

225 g/8 oz brown lentils
1 small onion, chopped
1 small leek, sliced
1 bay leaf

Dressing:
pinch dry mustard
30 ml/2 tbsp wine or cider vinegar
45 ml/3 tbsp unsaturated vegetable oil
1 shallot or small onion, finely chopped

freshly ground pepper

Croûtons:
30 ml/2 tbsp unsaturated vegetable oil
3 slices salt-free wholemeal bread (see page 94)
2 cloves garlic, crushed

Garnish:
chopped parsley

Put the lentils, onion, leek and bay leaf into a large pan. Add plenty of water, bring to the boil, reduce the heat, cover and simmer for 15–20 minutes, until the lentils are just tender but not mushy. Drain and cool.

To make the dressing, mix together the mustard and vinegar in a serving bowl. Add the oil and the shallot or onion. Season with pepper and stir in the lentils.

To make the croûtons, heat the oil in a pan, cut the bread into small cubes and fry in the hot oil with the crushed garlic until evenly brown.

Add to the lentil salad, and garnish with chopped parsley.

Rice salad

Serves 6
Each serving: negligible sodium; 8 mmol (298 mg) potassium; 214 Kcal

225 g/8 oz brown short-grain rice
3 tomatoes, chopped
1 green pepper, diced
1 red pepper, diced
1 handful unsalted roasted peanuts (see page 49)

Dressing:
30 ml/2 tbsp wine or cider vinegar

pinch dry mustard
pinch demerara sugar
45 ml/3 tbsp unsaturated vegetable oil
2 cloves garlic, finely chopped
5 ml/1 tsp mustard seeds
freshly ground pepper

Cook the rice in 575 ml/1 pint water for about 30 minutes, until just tender and all the water is absorbed. Cool, then place in a large serving bowl. Stir in the tomatoes, green and red pepper and peanuts.

To make the dressing, mix together the vinegar, mustard and sugar. Add the oil, chopped garlic, mustard seeds and pepper. Mix well. Pour the dressing over the rice and toss.

Celery, apple and walnut salad

Serves 4   See photograph, page 43
Each serving: 7 mmol (161 mg) sodium; 13 mmol (498 mg) potassium; 213 Kcal

Dressing:
45 ml/3 tbsp olive oil
30 ml/2 tbsp wine or cider vinegar
freshly ground pepper
30 ml/2 tbsp salt-free mayonnaise (see page 48)

Salad:
1 medium head celery, finely chopped
3 eating apples, cored and diced
50 g/2 oz walnuts, roughly chopped

Mix together the oil, vinegar and pepper. Stir in the mayonnaise. Add the celery, apples and walnuts and mix well.

VEGETABLE DISHES

Broad beans provençal

Serves 4
Each serving: 1 mmol (25 mg) sodium; 13 mmol (497 mg) potassium; 99 Kcal

15 ml/1 tbsp unsaturated vegetable oil
1 onion, sliced
2 cloves garlic, finely chopped
10 ml/2 tsp dried mixed herbs

4 tomatoes, sliced
900 g/2 lb broad beans, shelled
pinch chilli powder
freshly ground pepper

Heat the oil in a pan, add the onion, garlic and mixed herbs and cook over moderate heat for about 5 minutes. Stir in the tomatoes and broad beans, season with pepper and a pinch of chilli powder. Pour in 100 ml/3.5 fl oz water, cover and cook for 25–30 minutes, or until the broad beans are tender.

Braised red cabbage

Serves 4
Each serving: 4 mmol (84 mg) sodium; 21 mmol (815 mg) potassium; 98 Kcal

15 ml/1 tbsp unsaturated vegetable oil
1 medium-sized red cabbage, sliced
1 onion, finely chopped
1 small apple, sliced
30 ml/2 tbsp wine vinegar
freshly ground pepper

Heat the oil in a pan, add the cabbage, onion and apple and cook over moderate heat for about 5 minutes. Pour in 200 ml/7 fl oz water and the vinegar and season with pepper. Bring to the boil, reduce the heat, cover and cook for 35–40 minutes. Stir occasionally and add more water if necessary.

Swiss carrot and potato dish

Serves 4
Each serving: 5 mmol (118 mg) sodium; 24 mmol (931 mg) potassium; 165 Kcal

15 ml/1 tbsp unsaturated vegetable oil
1 large onion, finely chopped
450 g/1 lb carrots, peeled and cut into strips
450 g/1 lb medium size potatoes,
peeled and cut into quarters
freshly ground pepper

Garnish:
chopped parsley

Heat the oil in a pan, add the onion and cook over moderate heat for a few minutes, without browning. Stir in the carrots and potatoes. Pour in 50 ml/2 fl oz water, season with pepper, cover and simmer for 30–40 minutes, until the water is absorbed.

Turn into a serving dish and sprinkle with chopped parsley.

Spicy chick pea casserole

Serves 4
Each serving: 1 mmol (19 mg) sodium; 20 mmol (767 mg) potassium; 151 Kcal

100 g/4 oz chick peas
15 ml/1 tbsp unsaturated vegetable oil
1 large onion, finely chopped
3 cloves garlic, finely chopped
2 cm/1 in piece ginger root, peeled and finely chopped
or
2.5 ml/½ tsp ground ginger
5 ml/1 tsp cumin seeds
5 ml/1 tsp fennel seeds
5 ml/1 tsp mustard seeds
5 ml/1 tsp garam masala
2.5 ml/½ tsp chilli powder
1 green pepper, sliced
1 red pepper, sliced (optional)
2 aubergines, sliced
freshly ground pepper

Soak the chick peas overnight in cold water. Drain, then boil in plenty of salt-free water for about 2 hours until tender. Drain again.

Heat the oil in a pan, add the sliced onion, garlic and ginger and cook over moderate heat for 5–10 minutes, without browning. Add the cumin, fennel and mustard seeds and mix well. Stir in the chick peas, garam masala and chilli powder, then the sliced peppers and aubergines. Season with pepper. Pour in 150 ml/5 fl oz water, cover and cook slowly for 20–25 minutes.

Courgette casserole

Serves 4
Each serving: 4 mmol (99 mg) sodium; 7 mmol (280 mg) potassium; 146 Kcal

30 ml/2 tbsp unsaturated vegetable oil
675 g/1½ lb courgettes, thickly sliced
5 ml/1 tsp lemon juice
15 ml/1 tbsp chopped basil
freshly ground pepper
50 g/2 oz low-salt cheese, grated
50 g/2 oz salt-free wholemeal breadcrumbs (see page 96)

Heat the oven to 180°C/350°F/gas 4.

Heat half the oil in a pan, stir in the courgettes and cook over moderate heat for about 10 minutes. Remove from the heat, add the lemon juice and basil and season with pepper. Place half the courgettes in a baking dish and cover with half the cheese. Add the remaining courgettes and cheese. Fry the breadcrumbs in the remaining oil for a few minutes and sprinkle over the courgettes. Bake for about 40 minutes.

Serve hot.

Stuffed courgettes   See photograph, page 63

Serves 4
Each serving: 2 mmol (50 mg) sodium; 8 mmol (316 mg) potassium; 144 Kcal

4 medium size courgettes
15 ml/1 tbsp unsaturated vegetable oil
2 tomatoes, diced
225 g/8 oz fresh corn kernels
15 ml/1 tbsp chopped parsley
freshly ground pepper
25 g/1 oz low-salt cheese, grated

Heat the oven to 190°C/375°F/gas 5.

Cut the courgettes in half lengthwise and scoop out most of the flesh. Dice the flesh and keep aside for the stuffing. To make the stuffing, heat the oil in a pan, add the courgette flesh, tomatoes, corn kernels and chopped parsley and cook over moderate heat for 5–10 minutes, stirring occasionally. Season with pepper. Place the courgette shells in a baking dish, fill with the stuffing, sprinkle with grated cheese, pour 100 ml/3.5 fl oz water around the courgettes and bake for 20–25 minutes.

Serve hot.

Lentil curry

Serves 4

Each serving: 1 mmol (25 mg) sodium; 3 mmol (108 mg) potassium; 216 Kcal

15 ml/1 tbsp unsaturated vegetable oil
2 onions, finely chopped
2 cloves garlic, finely chopped
10 ml/2 tsp ground coriander
5 ml/1 tsp garam masala
5 ml/1 tsp turmeric
5 ml/1 tsp ground cumin

2.5 ml/½ tsp chilli powder
225 g/8 oz lentils
2 bay leaves
3 cloves
freshly ground pepper

Garnish:
fried onion rings

Heat the oil in a pan, add the onions, garlic and the coriander, garam masala, turmeric, cumin and chilli, and cook over moderate heat for 10 minutes, stirring occasionally. Stir in the lentils. Pour in 300 ml/10 fl oz water, add the bay leaves and cloves, season with pepper, cover and simmer for about 20 minutes, or until the lentils are just tender.

To make the garnish, fry the onion rings in a little vegetable oil and arrange on the lentils.

French onion tart

Serves 2–4

Each serving: 2–4 mmol (44–88 mg) sodium; 12–24 mmol (476–953 mg) potassium; 174–349 Kcal

Bread dough:
2.5 ml/½ tsp dried yeast
100 g/4 oz wholemeal flour

Filling:
15 ml/1 tbsp olive oil

450 g/1 lb onions, peeled and sliced
100 ml/3.5 fl oz skimmed milk
1 egg, beaten
freshly ground pepper
grated nutmeg
3 tomatoes, thinly sliced

To make the bread dough, pour approximately 100 ml/3.5 fl oz warm water into a small bowl and sprinkle on the yeast. Stir. Set aside in a warm place for 10–15 minutes, until frothy. Sift the flour into a mixing bowl, make a well in the centre, and pour in the yeast liquid. Mix to a firm dough, turn on to a lightly floured surface and knead until smooth. Cover loosely and leave in a warm place until doubled in size.

Heat the oven to 200°C/400°F/gas 6.

Grease a 28 cm/11 in pizza tray. Meanwhile, prepare the filling. Heat the oil in a pan, add the onions, cover and cook over moderate heat for about 20 minutes, stirring occasionally. Transfer the onions to a bowl, add the milk and the egg and mix well. Season with pepper and a little nutmeg. Knead the bread dough lightly, then roll it out thinly and line the pizza tray. Spread the onion mixture on the dough. Decorate with sliced tomatoes and bake for about 25 minutes, until golden brown.

Serve hot or cold.

Fried rice with vegetables

Serves 4

Each serving: 2 mmol (37 mg) sodium; 14 mmol (548 mg) potassium; 312 Kcal

225 g/8 oz brown short-grain rice
575 ml/1 pint salt-free, homemade stock (see page 45) or water
30 ml/2 tbsp unsaturated vegetable oil
2 carrots, finely sliced

1 small green pepper, finely sliced
1 leek, finely sliced
100 g/4 oz mushrooms, sliced
100 g/4 oz peas, fresh or frozen
freshly ground pepper

Cook the rice in the stock or water for about 30 minutes, until just tender and all the liquid is absorbed. Heat the oil in a pan, stir in the vegetables and cook for a few minutes. Add the rice, mix well and cook over moderate heat for about 10 minutes. Season with pepper.

Serve hot.

Tomatoes provençal

Serves 4

Each serving: negligible sodium; 16 mmol (611 mg) potassium; 45 Kcal

8 large tomatoes
25 g/1 oz fresh wholemeal salt-free breadcrumbs (see page 96)

1 shallot or small onion, finely chopped
1 clove garlic, crushed
10 ml/2 tsp dried mixed herbs

Cut a small round from the top of each tomato. Mix together the breadcrumbs, shallot or onion, garlic and mixed herbs. Put one teaspoon of the breadcrumb mixture on each tomato and put the tomatoes under a hot grill for about 5 minutes.

Stuffed courgettes (*top right*, see page 60), Tomatoes provençal (*top left*), Fried rice with vegetables (*bottom*)
OVERLEAF: Grilled stuffed fish (*top*, see page 71), Fish pie (*centre*, see page 69), Portuguese fish (*bottom*, see page 70)

Leek flan

Serves 4
Each serving: 2 mmol (54 mg) sodium; 17 mmol (667 mg) potassium; 344 Kcal

30 ml/2 tbsp unsaturated vegetable oil
450 g/1 lb leeks, cut into 1 cm/½ in pieces
1 large onion, sliced
25 g/1 oz plain flour
300 ml/½ pint skimmed milk
pinch ground nutmeg
freshly ground pepper
150 g/6 oz wholemeal pastry (see page 92)

Heat the oven to 180°C/350°F/gas 4.

Heat the oil in a pan, add the leeks and onion and cook over moderate heat for 15 minutes, without browning. Stir in the flour and gradually add the milk. Stir until the sauce thickens. Season with nutmeg and pepper. Cool slightly.

Grease a 20 cm/8 in flan ring. Roll out the pastry on a lightly floured surface and line the flan ring. Fill with the leek mixture and bake for about 30 minutes until the top is golden brown.

Serve hot or cold.

Stuffed tomatoes

Serves 4
Each serving: 1 mmol (21 mg) sodium; 19 mmol (734 mg) potassium; 100 Kcal

8 large tomatoes
100 g/4 oz cooked meat (beef, pork, lamb), minced
50 g/2 oz fresh wholemeal salt-free breadcrumbs (see page 96)
1 small onion, finely chopped
1 clove garlic, crushed
10 ml/2 tsp chopped chives
freshly ground pepper

Heat the oven to 180°C/350°F/gas 4.

Cut a small round from each tomato and scoop out the pulp. Mix together the meat, breadcrumbs, onion and garlic. Remove the pips from the tomato pulp, and add the pulp to the meat mixture with the chives. Season with pepper. Fill the tomatoes with the meat mixture, put on the lids and transfer to a baking dish. Pour 150 ml/3.5 fl oz water around the tomatoes and bake for 20–25 minutes.

Serve hot.

Leek flan (*top*), Potato galette (Rosti) (*centre*, see page 68), Potato cakes (*bottom*, see page 68)

Potato galette (Rosti)   See photograph, page 66

Serves 4
Each serving: negligible sodium; 34 mmol (1318 mg) potassium; 303 Kcal

900 g/2 lb potatoes, washed but not
  peeled
1 onion, finely chopped

freshly ground pepper
45 ml/3 tbsp unsaturated vegetable
  oil

Cook the potatoes in salt-free water for about 20 minutes, or until just tender, but still firm. Cool, then peel and grate the potatoes coarsely. Add the onion and season with pepper.

Heat the oil in a large frying pan, add the potato mixture, pressing it down with the back of a spoon. Fry the galette for about 10 minutes over moderate heat until the underside is golden brown. Turn it over by sliding it on to a plate and fry the other side.

When both sides are golden brown, turn on to a hot plate and serve in big chunky wedges.

Potato cakes   See photograph, page 66

Serves 4
Each serving: negligible sodium; 18 mmol (686 mg) potassium; 172 Kcal

450 g/1 lb hot cooked potatoes,
  mashed
50 g/2 oz wholemeal flour
freshly ground pepper

grated nutmeg
15 ml/1 tbsp unsaturated vegetable
  oil

Mix together the mashed potatoes and the flour. Season with pepper and some grated nutmeg. Make the potato cakes straight away to avoid change of colour. Heat the oil in a large frying pan. Shape the potato mixture into small round flat cakes and cook them for 5–10 minutes on each side. Serve hot.

New potatoes with garlic and chives

Serves 4
Each serving: 3 mmol (70 mg) sodium; 16 mmol (565 mg) potassium; 188 Kcal

15 ml/1 tbsp olive oil
675 g/1½ lb small new potatoes,
  washed but not peeled

2 cloves garlic, crushed
freshly ground pepper
15 ml/1 tbsp chopped chives

Heat the oil in a large heavy-based pan. Add the potatoes, cover and cook over a moderate heat for about 25 minutes, stirring occasionally. Add the garlic and cook for a further 5 minutes. Season with pepper, sprinkle with chopped chives and serve hot.

FISH

Fish fingers

Serves 4
Each serving: 5 mmol (106 mg) sodium; 15 mmol (590 mg) potassium; 164 Kcal

450 g/1 lb white fish fillets
1 bay leaf
225 g/8 oz cooked potatoes (optional)
freshly ground pepper

1 egg, beaten
50 g/2 oz salt-free fine wholemeal breadcrumbs (see page 96)

Put the fish in a pan with 45 ml/3 tbsp water and the bay leaf, cover and cook over moderate heat for about 15 minutes. Drain and cool. Mash the potatoes (if using). Remove the skin and any bone from the fish and flake the flesh. Mix together the fish and potato (if using) and season with pepper. Press the mixture on a lightly floured surface, cut into fingers, dip into the egg and coat with breadcrumbs. Grill for about 10 minutes on each side.

Fish pie
See photograph, page 64

Serves 4
Each serving: 6 mmol (130 mg) sodium; 21 mmol (814 mg) potassium; 222 Kcal

450 g/1 lb white fish fillets
300 ml/½ pint skimmed milk plus
  1 tbsp approximately
30 ml/2 tbsp unsaturated vegetable oil
25 g/1 oz plain flour

freshly ground pepper
225 g/8 oz cooked potatoes
100 g/4 oz mushrooms, sliced
50 g/2 oz salt-free wholemeal breadcrumbs – optional (see page 96)

Heat the oven to 190°C/375°F/gas 5.

Put the fish in a pan, add the milk, bring to the boil, reduce the heat and poach for 5 minutes. Drain and reserve the cooking liquid. Heat the oil in a pan, stir in the flour and gradually add the reserved liquid, stirring continuously until the sauce thickens. Season with pepper.

Mash the potatoes, adding a little skimmed milk if necessary. Flake the fish and arrange it in a baking dish. Add the mushrooms and pour the sauce over the fish. Pipe the creamed potatoes around the edge of the dish and sprinkle with breadcrumbs (if using).

Bake for about 20 minutes, until golden brown, and serve hot.

Portuguese fish

See photograph, page 65

Serves 4
Each serving: 6 mmol (140 mg) sodium; 26 mmol (1010 mg) potassium; 187 Kcal

450 g/1 lb tomatoes, sliced
2 onions, sliced
1 green pepper, sliced
15 ml/1 tbsp olive oil
2 cloves garlic, crushed

15 ml/1 tbsp chopped parsley
675 g/1½ lb piece of white fish
freshly ground pepper
100 ml/3.5 fl oz white wine or
* water*

Heat the oven to 180°C/350°F/gas 4.
   Place half the tomatoes, onions, and green pepper in a baking dish. Pour over the olive oil then add the garlic and parsley. Arrange the fish over the vegetables, season with pepper and cover with the remaining vegetables. Pour in the wine or water, cover with foil and bake for about 40 minutes.

Indian fried fish

Serves 4
Each serving: 6 mmol (130 mg) sodium; 14 mmol (550 mg) potassium; 188 Kcal

2.5 ml/½ tsp turmeric
2.5 ml/½ tsp chilli powder
1 clove garlic, crushed
675 mg/1½ lb white fish fillets

freshly ground pepper
25 g/1 oz plain flour
45 ml/3 tbsp unsaturated vegetable
* oil*

Mix together the turmeric, chilli powder and garlic. Divide the fish into 4 portions and press the garlic mixture into the fish. Season with pepper, then coat with flour. Heat the oil in a pan and fry the fish for about 5–10 minutes on each side until golden brown.

Fish German-style

Serves 4
Each serving: 6 mmol (137 mg) sodium; 18 mmol (721 mg) potassium; 172 Kcal

675 g/1½ lb piece of white fish (eg,
* cod, coley, haddock)*
25 g/1 oz medium oatmeal
15 ml/1 tbsp unsaturated vegetable
* oil*
2.5 ml/½ tsp dry mustard

15 g/1 tbsp chopped parsley
freshly ground pepper
10 ml/2 tsp lemon juice
15 ml/1 tbsp wine vinegar
100 g/4 oz mushrooms, sliced
1 small onion, chopped

Heat the oven to 190°C/375°F/gas 5.
   Cut the fish into 8 pieces and place in a baking dish. Mix

together the oatmeal, oil and mustard. Add the parsley and season with pepper. Spread the mixture over the fish. Mix together 100 ml/ 3.5 fl oz water, the lemon juice, vinegar, mushrooms and onion, and pour over the fish.

Cover the dish with foil and bake for about 25 minutes. Remove the foil and bake for a further 10 minutes.

Grilled stuffed fish
See photograph, page 65

Serves 4
Each serving: 6 mmol (134 mg) sodium; 18 mmol (683 mg) potassium; 150 Kcal

675 g/1½ lb bass, grey mullet or mackerel
1 onion, finely chopped
1 lemon

2 tomatoes, finely chopped
freshly ground pepper
10 ml/2 tsp chopped thyme
15 ml/1 tbsp olive oil

Stuff the fish with the chopped onion, half the lemon, peeled and finely sliced and the chopped tomatoes. Season with pepper. Sprinkle the thyme over the fish and season with more pepper. Pour over the juice of the remaining half lemon and the olive oil. Marinate for 2 hours. Cook the fish under a hot grill for about 15–20 minutes, turning once.

Baked fish

Serves 4
Each serving: 6 mmol (137 mg) sodium; 17 mmol (659 mg) potassium; 194 Kcal

12.5 g/½ oz unsalted butter
2 onions, finely chopped
15 ml/1 tbsp chopped parsley
675 g/1½ lb piece of cod, halibut or turbot
50 g/2 oz salt-free wholemeal bread-crumbs (see page 96)

100 ml/3.5 fl oz water and
100 ml/3.5 fl oz white wine
or
200 ml/7 fl oz water
freshly ground pepper

Heat the oven to 180°C/350°F/gas 4.

Spread the butter on the bottom of a baking dish. Arrange the onions and half the parsley in the dish. Place the fish on top. Sprinkle the breadcrumbs over the fish together with the remaining parsley. Pour in the water and white wine, if used, and season with pepper.

Cover with foil and bake for 20 minutes, basting occasionally. Remove the foil and bake for a further 10 minutes.

MEAT AND POULTRY

American beefburger

See photograph, page 75

Serves 4

Each serving: 4 mmol (99 mg) sodium; 9 mmol (354 mg) potassium; 253 Kcal

450 g/1 lb lean minced beef
1 small onion, finely chopped

10 ml/2 tsp mixed herbs, finely chopped
freshly ground pepper

Mix together the minced beef, onion, mixed herbs and freshly ground pepper. Divide the mixture into 4 large or 8 small equal portions and shape them into round flat cakes. Grill for about 10 minutes on each side.

Serve with a poached egg or a ring of pineapple. For a light meal, serve in a wholemeal roll (see page 95) filled with lettuce, sliced cucumber and tomato.

Spaghetti bolognese

Serves 4

Each serving: 4 mmol (104 mg) sodium; 20 mmol (793 mg) potassium; 638 Kcal

7.5 ml/½ tbsp unsaturated vegetable oil
1 small onion, chopped
2 cloves garlic, crushed
10 ml/2 tsp dried mixed herbs
450 g/1 lb lean minced beef
25 g/1 oz plain flour
575 ml/1 pint salt-free stock or *water*

450 g/1 lb tomatoes, chopped
or
400 g/14 oz canned tomatoes, chopped
a few fresh basil leaves (optional)
pinch chilli powder
freshly ground pepper
450 g/1 lb wholemeal spaghetti

Heat the oil in a pan, add the onion, garlic and mixed herbs and cook over moderate heat for 5–10 minutes, without browning. Add the minced beef and brown lightly all over. Stir in the flour, pour in the stock or water, add the tomatoes and basil leaves, if using, season with chilli and pepper and simmer, uncovered, for about 1 hour, stirring occasionally and adding more liquid if necessary. Keep warm or reheat when the spaghetti is ready.

Cook the spaghetti in plenty of unsalted water for 12–15 minutes. Drain, arrange in a warm serving dish and pour the bolognese sauce over it.

Serve with a green salad. Parmesan cheese, sprinkled over the spaghetti, should be avoided or used sparingly as any cheese contains a fair amount of salt.

Moussaká with courgettes

Serves 4
Each serving: 12 mmol (286 mg) sodium; 40 mmol (1566 mg) potassium; 484 Kcal

30 ml/2 tbsp unsaturated vegetable oil
2 onions, finely chopped
2 cloves garlic, finely chopped
5 ml/1 tsp dried mixed herbs
450 g/1 lb lamb or beef, minced
3 tomatoes, chopped
freshly ground pepper

575 ml/1 pint salt-free stock or water
450 g/1 lb courgettes, sliced
450 g/1 lb potatoes, peeled and thinly sliced
2 eggs
150 ml/5 fl oz low-fat plain yoghurt
50 g/2 oz Parmesan cheese, grated (optional)

Heat the oven to 180°C/350°F/gas 4.

Heat the oil in a pan, add the onions, garlic and mixed herbs and cook over low heat for a few minutes. Stir in the minced meat and chopped tomatoes and season with pepper. Add stock or water and cook over moderate heat for about 15 minutes.

In a large shallow baking dish arrange alternate layers of courgettes, potatoes and lamb mixture, finishing with a layer of potato. Bake for 35–40 minutes.

Meanwhile, beat together the eggs and the yoghurt, stir in the cheese if using, pour on to the moussaká and return to the oven for 15–20 minutes, until golden brown.

Beef croquettes

Serves 4
Each serving: 3 mmol (64 mg) sodium; 11 mmol (424 mg) potassium; 214 Kcal

350 g/12 oz cooked beef, minced
1 small onion, finely chopped
1 clove garlic, crushed
10 ml/2 tsp dried mixed herbs

100 g/4 oz wholemeal salt-free breadcrumbs – optional (see page 96)
5 ml/1 tsp paprika pepper
freshly ground pepper
1 egg, lightly beaten

Mix together the minced cooked beef, onion, garlic, mixed herbs, breadcrumbs, if using, paprika and pepper. Add the beaten egg to the beef mixture to bind it. Divide the mixture into 12 and shape into small flat round cakes. Grill for about 10 minutes on each side.

Serve with a spicy tomato sauce (see page 48).

Chilli con carne

Serves 4

Each serving: 5 mmol (109 mg) sodium; 28 mmol (1102 mg) potassium; 352 Kcal

225 g/8 oz dried kidney beans
15 ml/1 tbsp unsaturated vegetable oil
450 g/1 lb stewing beef, cut into 2 cm/ 1 in cubes
1 onion, finely chopped
3 cloves garlic, finely chopped
5 ml/1 tsp chilli powder
1 small green chilli, finely chopped (optional)

25 g/1 oz plain flour
400 ml/15 fl oz salt-free stock or *water*
100 ml/3.5 fl oz red wine (optional)
450 g/1 lb fresh tomatoes, chopped or *225 g/8 oz canned*
5 ml/1 tsp salt-free tomato purée
freshly ground pepper

Soak the kidney beans overnight in cold water.

Heat the oil in a pan and fry the beef cubes until evenly brown. Add the onion, garlic, chilli powder and chilli, if using, and continue cooking for a few minutes, stirring continuously. Stir in the flour. Gradually add the stock or water and wine, if using, the tomatoes and purée and season with pepper. Bring to the boil, reduce the heat, cover and simmer for about 2½ hours. Stir occasionally during cooking.

Meanwhile, cook the kidney beans in plenty of boiling unsalted water. It is important that the beans are properly boiled for 10 minutes; then cover and simmer for about 1 hour. Drain and add to the stew. Continue cooking until the beans are tender.

Serve with brown rice, couscous or cracked wheat.

Spiced lamb

Serves 4

Each serving: 8 mmol (180 mg) sodium; 19 mmol (676 mg) potassium; 65 Kcal

30 ml/2 tbsp unsaturated vegetable oil
675 g/1½ lb stewing lamb, boned and cut into cubes
small piece of cinnamon stick
1 bay leaf

4 cardamom pods
1 onion, finely chopped
6 cloves garlic, finely chopped
2 × 2 cm/1 in cubes ginger root, peeled and finely chopped

Chilli con carne (*top*), Spiced lamb (*centre*), American beefburger (*bottom*, see page 72)

25 g/1 oz plain flour
2.5 ml/½ tsp cayenne pepper

2.5 ml/½ tsp chilli powder
300 ml/½ pint plain low-fat yoghurt

Heat the oven to 180°C/350°F/gas 4.

Heat the oil in a pan and fry the lamb cubes, stirring continuously. Remove the meat and add to the pan the cinnamon, bay leaf and cardamom pods. Stir well. Add the onion, garlic and ginger. Cook over moderate heat for about 10 minutes. Add the meat, stir in the flour, then the cayenne pepper, chilli powder and yoghurt. Transfer the mixture to an ovenproof dish, cover and bake for about 1½ hours.

Pork kebabs

Serves 4
Each serving: 4 mmol (97 mg) sodium; 21 mmol (816 mg) potassium; 266 Kcal

Marinade:
2.5 ml/½ tsp mustard powder
15 ml/1 tbsp wine vinegar
30 ml/2 tbsp unsaturated vegetable oil
5 ml/1 tsp dried mixed herbs
1 clove garlic, finely chopped

freshly ground pepper

Kebabs:
450 g/1 lb pork, diced
1 small green pepper, cut into chunks
4 small onions, peeled and halved
4 tomatoes, halved

Make the marinade by mixing together the mustard, vinegar, oil, mixed herbs, garlic and pepper. Put the meat in a bowl, pour over the marinade, mix well and leave for about 4 hours in a cold place. Thread the diced meat, green pepper, onions and tomatoes alternately on 4 long skewers. Brush with the remaining marinade and cook under a hot grill for 15–20 minutes, turning occasionally.

Serve with brown rice and tomato sauce (see page 45) or stuffed inside pitta bread (see page 95) with lettuce and cucumber.

Crusty roast lamb

Serves 4
Each serving: 5 mmol (111 mg) sodium; 16 mmol (641 mg) potassium; 384 Kcal

1 small leg of lamb
2 cloves garlic, cut into small slivers
50 g/2 oz fresh wholemeal salt-free breadcrumbs (see page 96)
45 ml/3 tbsp chopped parsley

5 ml/1 tsp dried mixed herbs
15 ml/1 tbsp unsaturated vegetable oil
10 ml/2 tsp mustard powder
lemon juice

Crusty roast lamb (*top*), Pork kebabs (*bottom*)

Heat the oven to 190°C/375°F/gas 5.

Trim the joint, removing as much fat as possible from the top. Make several small incisions all over the lamb and insert a sliver of garlic into each one. Mix together the breadcrumbs, parsley and mixed herbs. Mix the oil and mustard and pour on to the breadcrumbs. Mix well. Spread the breadcrumb mixture all over the top and sides of the joint, pressing it down with your hands. Sprinkle with lemon juice and leave for 2 hours in a cold place.

Roast for about 1½–2 hours.

Rabbit fricassée

Serves 4

Each serving: 6 mmol (135 mg) sodium; 18 mmol (703 mg) potassium; 306 Kcal

30 ml/2 tbsp unsaturated vegetable oil
1.3 g/3 lb rabbit, jointed
1 large onion, finely chopped
1 carrot, scrubbed and sliced
2 cloves garlic
10 ml/2 tsp dried mixed herbs
freshly ground pepper
15 ml/1 tbsp plain flour
30 ml/2 tbsp wine or sherry

Heat the oil in a pan, add the rabbit pieces and brown all over. Add the onion and carrot and continue cooking on a low heat. Stir in the garlic and mixed herbs and season with pepper. Add the flour and mix well. Gradually stir in the wine or sherry and 850 ml/1½ pints water, cover and simmer for about 1½ hours, or until tender.

Chicken tandoori style

Serves 4

Each serving: 8 mmol (195 mg) sodium; 20 mmol (770 mg) potassium; 346 Kcal

8 chicken legs
1 large onion, minced or very finely chopped
4 cloves garlic, minced or very finely chopped
2 cm/1 in piece ginger root, peeled and minced or very finely chopped
10 ml/2 tsp chilli powder
10 ml/2 tsp coriander
5 ml/1 tsp ground cumin
60 ml/4 tbsp low-fat plain yoghurt
15 ml/1 tbsp lemon juice
15 ml/1 tbsp wine vinegar

Skin the chicken legs and put them in a baking dish. Mix together the onion, garlic and ginger. Add the chilli, coriander and cumin and mix well. Spread the spicy mixture over the chicken, pour over the yoghurt, lemon juice and vinegar and leave to marinate for about 4 hours.

Heat the oven to 180°C/350°F/gas 4.

Cover the dish with foil and bake for about 30 minutes. Remove the foil and bake for a further 10 minutes.

Roast chicken with herbs

Serves 4
Each serving: 12 mmol (275 mg) sodium; 28 mmol (1103 mg)
potassium; 501 Kcal

30 ml/2 tbsp unsaturated vegetable oil
1 clove garlic, finely chopped
10 ml/2 tsp dried mixed herbs
pinch mustard powder
150 ml/5 fl oz wine or water
freshly ground pepper
1.3 kg/3 lb chicken

Mix together the oil, garlic, mixed herbs, mustard powder, wine
or water and pepper. Put the chicken in a baking dish, pour the
marinade over it and leave for 1–2 hours, turning the chicken
occasionally.
   Heat the oven to 180°C/350°F/gas 4.
   Roast the chicken for about 1¼ hours, or until cooked
through.

Chicken with rice and velouté sauce

Serves 4   See photograph, page 41
Each serving: 14 mmol (314 mg) sodium; 42 mmol (1632 mg)
potassium; 708 Kcal

1.3 kg/3 lb chicken
1 large onion, peeled
2 carrots, peeled and diced
2 cloves
2 small leeks, cut in half
2 bay leaves
a few peppercorns
30 ml/2 tbsp unsaturated vegetable oil
225 g/8 oz brown short-grain rice

freshly ground pepper

Velouté sauce:
25 g/1 oz plain flour
1 clove garlic, crushed
10 ml/2 tsp dried mixed herbs
5 ml/1 tsp lemon juice

Garnish:
chopped parsley

Put the chicken into a large pan. Stick the cloves into the peeled
onion and add to the chicken together with the diced carrots,
leeks, bay leaves and peppercorns. Pour in 1.25 l/2¼ pints water,
bring to the boil, reduce the heat, cover and simmer for about 1¼
hours, or until the chicken is tender. Keep the chicken warm.
Strain the stock and use for the rice and the velouté sauce.
   Cook the rice: heat half the oil in a pan, add the rice and stir over
gentle heat for a few minutes. Add about half the strained chicken
stock taken from the chicken pan, season with pepper. Bring to
the boil, reduce the heat, cover and simmer for about 30 minutes,
or until the stock has been absorbed and the rice is just
tender.
   To make the velouté sauce, heat the remaining oil in a pan, stir
in the flour and gradually add the remaining strained stock, stirring continuously. Bring to the boil, reduce the heat, add the

garlic, mixed herbs and lemon juice. Season with pepper and continue cooking over gentle heat for 5–10 minutes.

Put the rice in a warm serving dish, carve the chicken and arrange it over the rice. Pour the sauce over the chicken and decorate with chopped parsley.

Chicken pie

Serves 4
Each serving: 2 mmol (51 mg) sodium; 12 mmol (452 mg) potassium; 584 Kcal

225 g/8 oz flaky pastry (see page 93)
15 ml/1 tbsp unsaturated vegetable oil
25 g/1 oz plain flour
550 ml/18 fl oz salt-free chicken stock (see page 45)
225 g/8 oz cooked chicken, diced
100 g/4 oz mushrooms, wiped and sliced
1 small red pepper, finely chopped
1 clove garlic, finely chopped
100 ml/3.5 fl oz white wine (optional)
freshly ground pepper
pinch chilli powder

Heat the oven to 190°C/375°F/gas 5.

Grease a 20 cm/8 in pie dish. Roll out half the pastry on a lightly floured surface and line the pie dish. Keep the other half of the pastry to cover the top.

Prepare the filling. Heat the oil in a pan, stir in the flour and gradually add the stock, stirring continuously, until the sauce thickens. Stir in the chicken, mushrooms, red pepper and garlic. Add the wine (if using). Season with pepper and a pinch of chilli powder. Cook for 5–10 minutes over moderate heat.

Spoon the chicken mixture into the pie case. Roll out the remaining pastry and cover the top, brushing the edges with water to seal them.

Bake for about 30 minutes, or until the pastry is lightly browned.

PUDDINGS

Fresh pineapple water ice

Serves 4   See photograph, page 87

Each serving: negligible sodium; 6 mmol (251 mg) potassium;
144 Kcal

100 g/4 oz sugar   *10 ml/2 tsp powdered gelatine*
1 fresh ripe pineapple, halved
  lengthwise

Heat 450 ml/¾ pint water and the sugar in a pan until the sugar has
dissolved. Bring to the boil and boil rapidly for a few minutes or
until the volume is reduced by a half. Cool.

Scoop out the flesh of the pineapple. Reserve the shells and chill
in the refrigerator until serving time. Purée the flesh in an electric
blender, or chop finely. Put 150 ml/¼ pint of the cooled syrup in a
bowl, stir in the gelatine and leave for a few minutes. Stand the
bowl in a pan of hot water and heat gently until the gelatine has
dissolved. Stir in the remaining syrup and leave until cold. Mix
together the syrup and pineapple purée, pour into a freezer con-
tainer, cover and freeze for 1–2 hours, until slushy.

Remove the mixture from the freezer, beat thoroughly and
return to the freezer for at least 2 hours, or until firm.

Stand the water ice at room temperature for about 15 minutes
to soften slightly, then scoop into the chilled pineapple shells.
Serve immediately.

Pear pie   See photograph, page 87

Serves 4

Each serving: negligible sodium; 7 mmol (282 mg) potassium;
503 Kcal

225 g/8 oz white shortcrust pastry (see   *50 g/2 oz walnuts, coarsely chopped*
  page 91)   *50 g/2 oz demerara sugar*
450 g/1 lb ripe pears, peeled and   *5 ml/1 tsp cinnamon*
  sliced   *a few drops vanilla essence*

Heat the oven to 180°C/350°F/gas 4.

Cut the pastry in half, then on a lightly floured surface roll out
one half and line a 23 cm/9 in pie tin. Place the fruit over the pastry.
Add the chopped walnuts and sprinkle with sugar, cinnamon and
vanilla essence. Dampen the edges of the pastry. Roll out the
remaining half, cover the pie and trim and pinch the edges to seal

them. Trimmings of pastry can be cut into leaf shapes and placed on top to decorate the pie. Bake for 30–35 minutes.
   Serve hot or cold.

Alternative   The potassium content is higher if wholemeal flour is used.

French plum flan   See photograph, page 41

Serves 6–8
Each serving: 1–2 mmol (25–33 mg) sodium; 8–10 mmol (296–394 mg) potassium; 283–378 Kcal

225 g/8 oz white shortcrust pastry (see   *50 g/2 oz granulated sugar*
   page 91)   *25 g/1 oz plain flour*
                                                   a few drops vanilla essence
Filling: *200 ml/7 fl oz skimmed milk*
900 g/2 lb ripe plums, stoned and cut
   in half   Topping:
1 egg   *25 g/1 oz demerara sugar*

Heat the oven to 180°C/350°F/gas 4.
   Roll out the pastry on a lightly floured surface and line a 28 cm/ 11 in tart tin. Arrange the fruit over the pastry.
   Mix together the egg and the sugar. Stir in the flour and vanilla essence and pour in the milk gradually, stirring continuously. Pour the custard over the fruit and bake for 35–40 minutes. Cool slightly and sprinkle with demerara sugar.
   Serve hot or cold.

Alternatives   The custard filling can be omitted. The potassium content is higher if wholemeal flour is used.

Summer fruit salad   See photograph, page 86

Serves 4
Each serving: negligible sodium; 13 mmol (503 mg) potassium; 118 Kcal

juice of 1 large orange   *225 g/8 oz strawberries, hulled and*
50 g/2 oz sugar   *sliced*
1 small melon, skinned, seeded and   *3 peaches, skinned, seeded and sliced*
   diced

Put the orange juice, sugar and 150 ml/¼ pint water in a pan and heat slowly until the sugar has dissolved. Bring to the boil and boil rapidly for a few minutes, until syrupy. Cool
   Put the fruit in a serving bowl, pour over the cool syrup and mix gently.
   Serve as soon as possible.

Winter fruit salad

Serves 4
Each serving: negligible sodium; 26 mmol (605 mg) potassium; 246 Kcal

50 g/2 oz sugar
2 oranges, peeled, sliced and seeded
225 g/8 oz seedless green grapes, halved
2 bananas, peeled and sliced

2 eating apples
juice of ½ lemon
50 g/2 oz walnuts
15 ml/1 tbsp kirsch (optional)

Put 150 ml/¼ pint water and the sugar in a pan and heat over moderate heat until the sugar has dissolved. Bring to the boil and boil rapidly for a few minutes, until syrupy. Cool.

Put the oranges, grapes and bananas in a serving bowl. Peel, core and slice the apples and sprinkle with lemon juice to prevent discoloration. Add to the other fruit together with the walnuts. Pour over the cool syrup, add the kirsch, if using, and mix gently.

Serve as soon as possible.

Savarin

See photograph, page 86

Serves 4–6
Each serving: 2–3 mmol (52–77 mg) sodium; 6–8 mmol (220–331 mg) potassium; 399–599 Kcal

Batter:
30 ml/2 tbsp sugar
300 ml/½ pint warm skimmed milk
12.5 g/½ oz dried yeast
250 g/9 oz strong plain white flour
100 g/4 oz polyunsaturated salt-free margarine, melted

2 eggs, beaten

Filling:
100 g/4 oz sugar
fresh fruit, eg, strawberries, raspberries, pineapple, peaches

To make the batter, dissolve 5 ml/1 teaspoon of the sugar in the warm milk. Sprinkle on the yeast, stir and leave in a warm place for 10–15 minutes, until the liquid becomes frothy. Place the flour and remaining sugar in a large bowl. Make a well in the centre, pour in the melted margarine and the yeast liquid, add the beaten eggs, and beat with a wooden spoon for about 5 minutes.

Heat the oven to 200°C/400°F/gas 6.

Turn the batter into a greased and floured 23 cm/9 in savarin mould and leave in a warm place for 10 minutes.

Bake for about 35 minutes, until golden and well risen. Cool.

To make the filling, dissolve the sugar in 150 ml/¼ pint water over low heat. Bring to the boil and boil for a few minutes. Pour over the savarin.

Prepare the fruit and pile in the centre. Serve soon after adding the fruit.

Orange and date fruit salad

Serves 4
Each serving: negligible sodium; 8 mmol (297 mg) potassium;
257 Kcal

50 g/2 oz sugar
1.25 ml/¼ tsp vanilla essence
2 oranges, peeled, sliced into rings and seeded

75 g/3 oz whole dates, stoned and chopped
2 eating apples
juice of ½ lemon
50 g/2 oz flaked almonds

Place the sugar, 150 ml/¼ pint water and the vanilla essence in a pan and heat slowly until the sugar has dissolved. Bring to the boil and boil rapidly for a few minutes, until syrupy. Cool.

Put the oranges and dates in a serving bowl. Core the apples, then slice them and sprinkle with lemon juice to prevent discoloration. Add to the fruit in the bowl. Pour over the sugar syrup.

Put the flaked almonds under a hot grill for a few minutes, then sprinkle over the orange salad.

Serve as soon as possible.

PASTRY AND BAKING

Orange chocolate cake

Makes 8 slices
Each slice: 1 mmol (19 mg) sodium; 3 mmol (109 mg) potassium;
350 Kcal

100 g/4 oz polyunsaturated salt-free margarine
100 g/4 oz sugar
2 eggs, beaten
50 g/2 oz plain chocolate, grated

30 ml/2 tbsp fresh orange juice
50 g/2 oz walnuts, chopped (optional)
125 g/5 oz plain white flour
5 ml/1 tsp baking powder substitute (see page 96)

Orange chocolate cake (*top*), Orange and date fruit salad (*centre and bottom*)
OVERLEAF: Savarin (*top left*, see page 83), Pear pie (*top right*, see page 81), Summer fruit salad (*bottom left and centre*, see page 82), Fresh pineapple water ice (*bottom right*, see page 81)

Icing:
175 g/6 oz icing sugar
30 ml/2 tbsp fresh orange juice

peel of 1 orange, cut into julienne strips
and blanched

Heat the oven to 180°C/350°F/gas 4.

Beat together the margarine and sugar until light and fluffy. Add the eggs gradually, beating well after each addition. Stir in the grated chocolate and fresh orange juice. Add the walnuts, if using. Sift the flour with the baking powder substitute and stir into the egg mixture.

Pour into a greased 18 cm/7 in round cake tin and bake for 30–40 minutes, or until a skewer pierced through the centre comes out clean. Cool before turning out. Make up the icing with the orange juice, pour over the cake and decorate with the peel.

Almond cake

Makes 12 slices
Each slice: 1 mmol (18 mg) sodium; 3 mmol (108 mg) potassium; 249 Kcal

175 g/6 oz polyunsaturated salt-free
  margarine
175 g/6 oz sugar
3 eggs, beaten
175 g/6 oz plain flour

5 ml/1 tsp baking powder substitute
  (see page 96)
100 g/4 oz ground almonds
1.25 ml/¼ tsp almond essence

Decoration:
icing sugar

Heat the oven to 180°C/350°/gas 4.

Beat together the margarine and the sugar until light and fluffy. Add the eggs, a little at a time, and beat well after each addition. Sift together the flour and baking powder substitute, add the ground almonds and the almond essence and gradually stir into the egg mixture.

Pour the mixture into a greased 20 cm/7½ in cake tin and bake for about 40 minutes, or until a skewer pierced through the centre comes out clean.

Cool in the tin before turning it out, then sprinkle icing sugar over the top.

An alternative The potassium content can be increased by using wholemeal flour instead of white.

Almond cake (*top*), Two-cereal bread (*centre*, see page 94), Sesame fingers (*bottom*, see page 90)

Shortbread

Makes about 16 biscuits
Each biscuit: negligible sodium; negligible potassium; 93 Kcal

100 g/4 oz plain white flour
50 g/2 oz rice flour
50 g/2 oz sugar
100 g/4 oz unsalted butter

Decoration:
5 ml/1 tsp caster sugar

Heat the oven to 170°C/325°F/gas 3.
   Sift the flours into a bowl and add the sugar. Cut the butter into small pieces and gradually work it into the dry ingredients until like a smooth dough. Transfer to a 18 cm/7 in square or round tin. Bake for about 30 minutes, until lightly golden.
   Sprinkle the caster sugar on top and cool in the tin for a few minutes. Cut into small fingers and cool completely before removing from the tin.

An alternative   The potassium content could be increased if wholemeal flour were used instead of white flour.

Digestive biscuits

Makes about 24
Each biscuit: negligible sodium; 1 mmol (40 mg) potassium; 61 Kcal

175 g/6 oz wholemeal flour
50 g/2 oz fine oatmeal
5 ml/1 tsp baking powder substitute
*   (see page 96)*

75 g/3 oz polyunsaturated salt-free
*   margarine*
25 g/1 oz demerara sugar
60 ml/4 tbsp skimmed milk,
*   approximately*

Heat the oven to 190°C/375°F/gas 5.
   Mix together the flour, oatmeal and baking powder substitute. Rub in the margarine until the mixture looks like breadcrumbs, then stir in the sugar. Add the milk and mix to a firm dough. Turn on to a lightly floured surface and roll out thinly, then cut into 6 cm/2½ in rounds. Prick over with a fork a few times. Transfer to a greased baking tray and bake for about 15–20 minutes.
   Cool on a rack.

Sesame fingers

See photograph, page 88

Makes about 24
Each biscuit: negligible sodium; 1 mmol (45 mg) potassium; 88 Kcal

175 g/6 oz medium oatmeal
50 g/2 oz sesame seeds, roasted
90 ml/6 tbsp unsaturated vegetable
*   oil*

45 ml/3 tbsp clear honey
50 g/2 oz demerara sugar

Heat the oven to 180°C/350°F/gas 4.

Mix all the ingredients together. Press into a well greased Swiss roll tin and smooth the top. Bake for about 20 minutes. Cool in the tin for a few minutes, then cut into fingers and cool completely before removing from the tin.

Apple cake

Makes 8 slices
Each slice: 1 mmol (20 mg) sodium; 4 mmol (138 mg) potassium; 167 Kcal

2 eggs
75 g/3 oz sugar
75 g/3 oz plain white flour
2.5 ml/½ tsp baking powder substitute
 (see page 96)

50 g/2 oz demerara sugar
25 g/1 oz polyunsaturated salt-free
 margarine
10 ml/2 tsp cinnamon

For the layers:
675 g/1½ lb cooking apples, peeled
 and sliced

Heat the oven to 180°C/350°F/gas 4.

Beat together the eggs and the sugar until light and creamy. Sift the flour and baking powder substitute and fold into the egg mixture. Pour the mixture into a greased 18 cm/7 in round cake tin.

Divide the apples, sugar, margarine and cinnamon into 3 parts and arrange a third of the apples on the dough. Sprinkle with a third of the sugar, cinnamon and margarine, cut into small flakes. Repeat twice. Bake for 40–45 minutes.

An alternative Potassium content will be increased by 7 mmol per slice if wholemeal flour is used.

Shortcrust pastry (using margarine only)

Per ¼ recipe: negligible sodium; 2 mmol (80 mg) potassium; 380 Kcal

225 g/8 oz plain white flour
100 g/4 oz salt-free polyunsaturated
 margarine

Place the flour in a bowl. Cut the margarine into small pieces and add to the flour. Rub the margarine into the flour until it looks like fresh breadcrumbs. Add approximately 90 ml/6 tbsp cold water gradually and mix to a soft, smooth dough. If it is sticky, add a little flour. The pastry can be used straight away.

Shortcrust pastry (using oil and margarine)

Per ¼ recipe: negligible sodium; 2 mmol (79 mg) potassium; 356 Kcal

225 g/8 oz plain white flour
50 g/2 oz polyunsaturated salt-free margarine

30 ml/2 tbsp unsaturated vegetable oil

Place the flour in a bowl. Cut the margarine into small pieces and add to flour. Rub the margarine into the flour until it looks like fresh breadcrumbs. Add the oil and mix well. Pour in approximately 90 ml/6 tbsp cold water gradually and mix to a soft, smooth dough. The pastry can be used straight away.

Wholemeal pastry (using margarine only)

Per ¼ recipe: negligible sodium; 5 mmol (204 mg) potassium; 362 Kcal

225 g/8 oz wholemeal flour
100 g/4 oz salt-free polyunsaturated margarine

Place the flour in a bowl. Cut the margarine into small pieces and add to the flour. Rub the margarine into the flour until it looks like fresh breadcrumbs. Add approximately 90 ml/6 tbsp cold water gradually and mix to a soft, smooth dough. The pastry is best chilled for 30 minutes before using.

Wholemeal pastry (using oil and margarine)

Per ¼ recipe: negligible sodium; 5 mmol (204 mg) potassium; 371 Kcal

225 g/8 oz wholemeal flour
50 g/2 oz polyunsaturated salt-free margarine

45 ml/3 tbsp unsaturated vegetable oil

Place the flour in a bowl. Cut the margarine into small pieces and add to flour. Rub the margarine into the flour until it looks like fresh breadcrumbs. Add the oil and mix well. Pour in approximately 90 ml/6 tbsp cold water, a little at a time, and mix to a soft, smooth dough. The pastry is best chilled for 30 minutes before using.

Flaky pastry

Per ¼ recipe: negligible sodium; 2 mmol (80 mg) potassium;
425 Kcal

125 g/5 oz polyunsaturated salt-free   225 g/8 oz plain flour
  margarine

Divide the margarine into 4 equal portions. Place the flour in a
bowl and rub one quarter of the margarine into it until it re-
sembles fresh breadcrumbs. Mix to a soft dough with approximately 120 ml/8 tbsp cold water.

On a lightly floured surface roll the pastry into an oblong. Put
another quarter of the margarine over it, cut into small flakes.
Fold the bottom third up and the top third of the pastry down, seal
the edges and turn it so that the folds are now at the sides. Roll
again, put another quarter of margarine over it and repeat in the
same way until all the margarine has been used up. Leave the pastry
in the refrigerator at least 30 minutes before using.

BREADMAKING

As any bread bought at the baker contains salt it is important that
you should try to bake your own bread. With a little practice
breadmaking becomes easy provided you follow a few simple
rules.

- When baking wholemeal bread make sure that you use 100
  per cent stoneground wholemeal flour to ensure that it is
  salt-free.
- Dissolve the dried yeast in warm water or milk (43°C/110°F)
  and leave in a warm place for about 10 minutes, until frothy.
  A little sugar in the water helps the yeast to activate.

  Dried yeast has been used for all the bread recipes in this
  book as fresh yeast is more difficult to find and keeps for
  only a few days. If, however, you wish to use fresh yeast you
  will need twice the quantity of dried yeast.
- When the yeast is frothy, add to the flour and other
  ingredients and mix to a dough. Transfer the dough to a
  lightly floured surface and knead for 5–10 minutes.
- Place the dough in a lightly floured bowl, cover loosely and
  leave in a warm place until it has doubled in size. Depending
  on the kind of dough and the ingredients used it will take
  between 30 minutes and 1½ hours.
- Knead the dough once again, then shape and transfer to a
  greased baking tin or tray and cover loosely.
- Leave to rise again. This will usually take between 15 and
  30 minutes.
- Bake in a hot oven.

Wholemeal bread

Makes 1 loaf, 12 slices
Each slice: negligible sodium; 6 mmol (145 mg) potassium; 133 Kcal

5 ml/1 tsp sugar
10 ml/2 tsp dried yeast
450 g/1 lb wholemeal flour

30 ml/2 tbsp bran
12.5 g/½ oz salt-free polyunsaturated
  margarine

Dissolve the sugar in 150 ml/5 fl oz lukewarm water. Sprinkle on the yeast, stir well and leave in a warm place for 10 minutes, until frothy. Place the flour and bran in a large bowl and rub in the margarine. Pour in the frothy yeast liquid and approximately 100 ml/3.5 fl oz lukewarm water. Mix to a dough, adding more flour if necessary. Transfer to a lightly floured surface and knead for 5–10 minutes, until smooth and elastic. Cover loosely and leave in a warm place until it has doubled in size.

Turn out the dough and knead again for a few minutes. Grease a 450 g/1 lb loaf tin and shape the dough to fit the tin. Leave covered in a warm place for about 30 minutes.

Heat the oven to 220°C/425°F/gas 7 and bake the bread for 30–40 minutes, until golden brown and sounds hollow when tapped underneath.

Cool on a wire tray.

Two-cereal bread   See photograph, page 88

Makes 2 loaves, 12 slices each
Each slice: negligible sodium; 4 mmol (149 mg) potassium; 133 Kcal

5 ml/1 tsp sugar
20 ml/4 tsp dried yeast
675 g/1½ lb wholemeal flour
225 g/8 oz rye flour
60 ml/4 tbsp bran

25 g/1 oz salt-free polyunsaturated
  margarine

Decoration:
kibbled wheat

Dissolve the sugar in 150 ml/¼ pint lukewarm water. Sprinkle on the yeast, stir well and leave in a warm place for 10 minutes, until frothy.

Put the flours and bran in a large bowl and rub in the margarine. Pour in the frothy yeast liquid and approximately 450 ml/¾ pint lukewarm water. Mix to a dough, adding more flour if necessary. Transfer to a lightly floured surface and knead for 5–10 minutes until smooth and elastic. Cover lightly and leave in a warm place until it has doubled in size.

Turn out the dough and knead again for a few minutes. Grease 2 baking trays. Divide the dough into two and shape each one into a ball. Place on the baking trays. Score the loaves with a sharp knife in a lattice pattern, brush with water and sprinkle with kibbled wheat. Leave covered in a warm place for about 30 minutes.

Heat the oven to 220°C/425°F/gas 7 and bake the bread for 40–50 minutes.

Cool on a wire tray.

Breakfast rolls

Makes 12
Each roll: negligible sodium; 4 mmol (160 mg) potassium; 204 Kcal

5 ml/1 tsp sugar
15 ml/3 tsp dried yeast
450 g/1 lb wholemeal flour
225 g/8 oz white strong flour

25 g/1 oz salt-free polyunsaturated margarine

Decoration:
sesame seeds

Dissolve the sugar in 150 ml/¼ pint lukewarm water. Sprinkle on the yeast, stir well and leave in a warm place for 10 minutes, until frothy.

Place the flours in a large bowl and rub in the margarine. Pour in the frothy yeast liquid and approximately 300 ml/½ pint water and mix to a dough, adding more flour if necessary. Transfer to a lightly floured surface and knead for 5–10 minutes until smooth and elastic. Cover lightly and leave in a warm place until it has doubled in size.

Turn out the dough and knead again for a few minutes. Grease a large baking tray. Divide the dough into 12 pieces and shape each one into a round cake. Brush with water and sprinkle with sesame seeds. Leave covered in a warm place for about 30 minutes.

Heat the oven to 220°C/425°F/gas 7 and bake the bread for about 20 minutes until golden brown.

Cool on a wire tray.

Pitta bread

Makes 8
Each pitta: negligible sodium; 4 mmol (138 mg) potassium; 189 Kcal

5 ml/1 tsp sugar
10 ml/2 tsp dried yeast

225 g/8 oz wholemeal flour
225 g/8 oz strong white flour

Dissolve the sugar in 150 ml/¼ pint lukewarm water. Sprinkle on the yeast, stir well and leave in a warm place for 10 minutes, until frothy.

Place the flours in a large bowl and pour in the frothy yeast liquid and approximately 100 ml/3.5 fl oz lukewarm water. Mix to a dough, adding more flour if necessary. Transfer to a lightly floured surface and knead for 5–10 minutes, until smooth and elastic. Cover lightly and leave in a warm place until it has doubled in size.

Turn out the dough and knead again for a few minutes. Grease 2 baking trays. Divide the dough into 8 pieces and shape each one into a smooth, seamless ball. Space the pitta balls on a floured surface and allow to rest, covered, for 10 minutes.

Heat the oven to 220°C/425°F/gas 7. Flatten 2 or 3 balls into ovals 20 cm/8 in long, lift them on to a greased baking tray and bake for 5–10 minutes until lightly browned.

Repeat the process until all the pittas are baked.

NB Do not flatten the other balls until there is room in the oven for them to be baked as they will rise prematurely and be difficult to handle.

Serving suggestions   Pittas are usually halved, split open and filled with salad and meat.

Breadcrumbs

per 25 g/1 oz wholemeal fresh: negligible sodium; 1 mmol (55 mg) potassium; 54 Kcal

per 25 g/1 oz white fresh: negligible sodium; 1 mmol (55 mg) potassium; 58 Kcal

Leftover salt-free wholemeal or white
  bread

Heat the oven to 170°C/325°F/gas 3.

Put the bread in an electric blender or coffee grinder and switch it on for a few minutes. The bread can also be crumbled by hand. Place the crumbs on a baking tray and bake for 15–20 minutes, stirring occasionally. Cool and store in an airtight tin.

Alternatives   For fine breadcrumbs, rub the baked crumbs through a sieve.

For fresh breadcrumbs, omit the baking process.

Baking powder substitute

To be made by a chemist:

potassium bicarbonate 39.8 g   *tartaric acid 7.5 g*
starch 28.0 g   *potassium bitartrate 56.1 g*

Use 1 heaped tsp per 225 g/8 oz plain flour.

An alternative   Use Salfree baking powder, which is available from some health shops or direct from Cantassium Company Limited, Larkhall Laboratories, 225 Putney Bridge Road, London SW15 2PY.

Wholemeal scones

Makes about 12
Each scone: negligible sodium; 2 mmol (68 mg) potassium; 32 Kcal

225 g/8 oz plain wholemeal flour
5 ml/1 tsp baking powder substitute
(see above)

50 g/2 oz polyunsaturated salt-free margarine
skimmed milk for glazing

Heat the oven to 220°C/425°F/gas 7.

Sift the flour and baking powder substitute into a bowl. Rub in the margarine until the mixture looks like breadcrumbs. Add approximately 90 ml/6 tbsp cold water gradually and mix to a soft dough. Turn on to a lightly floured surface and roll out to a 2 cm/¾ in thickness. Cut into 5 cm/2 in rounds and brush with a little skimmed milk. Transfer to a floured baking tray and bake for 10–15 minutes.

Cool on a rack.

Date and apple scones

Makes about 12
Each scone: negligible sodium; 1 mmol (46 mg) potassium; 109 Kcal

225 g/8 oz plain white flour
5 ml/1 tsp baking powder substitute
(see page 96)
2.5 ml/½ tsp mixed spice
50 g/2 oz polyunsaturated salt-free margarine

25 g/1 oz demerara sugar
50 g/2 oz dates, chopped
1 small cooking apple (125 g/4 oz), peeled and grated
45 ml/3 tbsp skimmed milk, approximately

Heat the oven to 220°C/425°F/gas 7.

Sift the flour, baking powder substitute and mixed spice into a bowl. Rub in the margarine until it looks like breadcrumbs. Add the sugar, dates and apple and mix well. Add the milk gradually and mix to a soft dough. Turn on to a lightly floured surface and roll out to a 2 cm/¾ in thickness. Cut into 5 cm/2 in rounds. Transfer to a floured baking tray and bake for 10–15 minutes.

Cool on a rack.

The sodium and potassium content of common foods

Vegetables

NB All vegetables cooked are without salt

	Wt (g)	Handy measure	Sodium mmol	Potassium mmol	Kcal
Asparagus	120	6 Spears	Tr	3.7	11
Beans, baked – canned in tomato sauce	200	5 heaped tablespoons	41.7	15.4	128
Beans, broad, boiled	100	4 rounded tablespoons	0.9	5.9	48
Beans, red kidney, uncooked	30	2 level tablespoons	0.5	8.9	82
Beans, runner, boiled	100	4 rounded tablespoons	Tr	3.8	19
Beetroot, boiled	50	3 slices *or* 1 small	1.4	4.5	22
Broccoli, boiled	100	5 small spears	0.3	5.6	18
Brussels sprouts, boiled	100	14 medium	0.1	6.2	18
Cabbage, red, raw	120	⅛ medium *or* 1 cup, shredded	1.7	9.2	24
Cabbage, spring, boiled	100	4 rounded tablespoons	0.5	2.8	7
Carrots, old, boiled	100	4 rounded tablespoons	2.2	2.2	19
Cauliflower, boiled	100	3 large florets	0.2	4.6	9
Celery, raw	60	1 large stick	3.6	4.3	5
Celery, cooked	100	4 rounded tablespoons	2.9	3.3	5
Leeks, boiled	150	1 medium	0.4	10.8	36
Lentils, uncooked	60	4 level tablespoons	0.9	10.3	182
Lettuce, raw	15	2 large leaves	0.1	0.9	2
Marrow, boiled	200	¼ medium	0.1	4.3	14
Mushrooms, raw	60	4 medium button	0.2	7.2	8
Onions, raw	50	1 small	0.2	1.8	11
Parsnips, boiled	120	1 medium	0.2	8.9	67
Peas, canned, garden	100	4 rounded tablespoons	10.1	3.3	47
Peas, frozen, boiled	100	4 rounded tablespoons	0.1	3.3	41
Peppers, green raw	30	¼ medium	Tr	1.6	4
Plantain, green, boiled	60	5 cm/2 in piece	0.1	5.1	73
Potato, baked, jacket	150	1 medium	0.5	26.1	158
Potato, boiled	50	1 small – egg size	0.1	4.2	40
Potato, chips	70	1 cup	0.4	18.3	177
Potato, crisps, salted	25	1 small packet	6.0	7.6	133
Potato, instant, made-up	50	1 rounded tablespoon	5.6	4.4	35

	Wt (g)	Handy measure	Sodium mmol	Potassium mmol	Kcal
Radish	8	1 medium	0.2	0.5	1
Spinach, boiled	100	4 rounded tablespoons	5.2	12.6	30
Sweetcorn, canned kernels	100	4 rounded tablespoons	13.5	5.1	76
Sweetcorn, on the cob	200	1 medium cob	Tr	7.2	123
Sweet potato, boiled	60	size of a large egg	0.5	4.6	51
Tomato, raw	80	1, diameter 5 cm/2 in	0.1	6.0	11
Yam, boiled	100	½ slice, 3.5 cm/1½ in thick	0.7	7.7	119

Fruit

	Wt (g)	Handy measure	Sodium mmol	Potassium mmol	Kcal
Apple, cooking, stewed with sugar	100	½ cup	0.1	2.4	66
Apple, eating	120	1 medium	0.1	3.7	42
Apricots, raw	90	3 medium	Tr	6.7	22
Apricots, dried	20	6 halves	0.5	9.6	36
Avocado pear	120	½ medium	0.1	12.3	268
Banana	170	18 cm/7 in piece with skin	0.1	9.2	80
Blackberries, raw	25	10 medium	Tr	1.3	7
Cherries, eating	80	10 large	0.1	4.9	33
Currants, black, raw	25	1 rounded tablespoon	Tr	2.4	7
Dates, dried	30	5 without stones	0.1	5.0	74
Figs, raw	50	1	Tr	3.5	20
Figs, dried	20	1	0.8	5.2	43
Fruit salad, canned	150	1 cup	0.1	4.6	142
Grapes	80	10 large	Tr	5.2	41
Grapefruit, fresh	150	½ medium	0.1	8.8	33
Lychees, raw	120	8 with skin	0.2	5.2	77
Mangoes, raw	400	1 medium	1.2	19.5	236
Melon, honeydew	200	⅙ medium	1.0	7.2	26
Nectarine, raw	100	1 medium	0.3	6.4	46
Olives in brine	4	1 without stone	3.9	0.1	4
Orange	150	1 medium	0.1	5.8	39
Peach	100	1 medium	0.1	5.9	32
Pear	140	1 medium	Tr	3.4	41
Pineapple, fresh	50	1 slice – small fruit	0.1	3.2	23
Plums, dessert, raw	90	2 medium	0.1	4.2	32
Prunes, dried	50	5	0.2	9.2	68
Raisins	25	1 rounded tablespoon	0.6	5.5	62
Raspberries	25	10 medium	Tr	1.4	6
Rhubarb, raw	100	1 stick	0.1	11.0	6
Strawberries	100	10 medium	0.1	4.1	26
Sultanas	25	1 rounded tablespoon	0.6	5.5	62
Tangerines	100	1 medium	0.1	2.8	23

Meat and fish

	Wt (g)	Handy measure	Sodium mmol	Potassium mmol	Kcal
Meat					
Bacon, grilled, lean only	30	1 rasher	29.2	2.7	88
Beef, minced, raw weight	120	2 heaped tablespoons	4.5	8.9	265
Beef, rump steak, grilled, lean only	200	12 × 10 × 1 cm/5 × 4 × ½ in	4.9	20.5	336
Beef, topside roast, lean only	100	3 thin slices	2.1	4.5	156
Chicken joint	250	¼ small bird	4.5	10.3	185
Chicken, roast, no skin	100	3 thin slices, 10 × 5 cm/4 × 2 in	3.5	7.9	148
Corned beef, canned	80	2 large thin slices	33.0	2.9	174
Frankfurter	45	1 large	19.2	1.1	122
Gammon, boiled	90	3 thin slices	43.4	5.8	150
Lamb, chop, lean only	90	1 medium 1 cm/½ in thick	2.2	5.8	122
Lamb, leg, roast, lean only	100	3 thin slices 10 × 7 cm/4 × 3 in	2.9	8.7	191
Liver, lamb's, raw weight	100	3 medium slices	3.3	7.4	179
Meat curry, with salt	200	1 cup	41.7	10.8	320
Pork, chop, lean only	100	1 medium, 12 × 1 cm/ 5 × ½ in thick	2.2	6.4	133
Pork, leg, roast, lean only	100	2 medium slices 10 × 7 × 1 cm/4 × 3 × ½ in	3.4	10.0	185
Pork pie, bought	150	Individual	47.0	5.8	564
Salami	30	4 small thin slices	24.1	1.2	147
Sausage, beef	45	1	21.5	2.2	119
Sausage, pork	45	1	19.6	2.3	143
Sausage roll, bought	120	1 × 12 cm/5 in long	28.7	3.4	575
Steak and kidney pie, bought	240	Individual	53.2	8.6	775
Tongue, canned	80	2 large thin slices	36.5	2.0	170
Fish					
Cockles, boiled in salt water	15	5 medium	23.0	0.2	7
Cod, fried in batter	200	1 medium fillet	8.7	19.0	398
Cod, raw	180	1 medium fillet	6.0	14.8	137
Crab, boiled	100	2 heaped tablespoons	16.1	6.9	127
Fish fingers, bought	25	1 finger	3.5	1.5	44
Haddock, smoked	180	1 medium fillet	61.8	8.8	119
Mussels, boiled without salt	25	3 medium	2.3	0.6	22
Plaice	100	1 medium fillet	5.2	7.2	91
Prawns, peeled	60	2 heaped tablespoons	41.5	4.0	64
Sardine, canned	20	1	5.7	2.2	43
Tuna, canned in oil	100	2 heaped tablespoons	18.3	7.2	289

Dairy products

	Wt (g)	Handy measure	Sodium mmol	Potassium mmol	Kcal
Cheese					
Camembert type	45	Individual portion, ¹/₆ of 10 cm/4 in round	27.6	1.3	135
Cheddar type	45	5 × 2.5 × 1 cm/2 × 1 × ½ in	11.9	1.4	183
Cheese spread	11	1 triangle	5.6	0.4	31
Cottage cheese	120	2 heaped tablespoons	23.5	1.7	115
Cream cheese	45	3 level tablespoons	5.9	1.8	198
Edam type	45	5 × 2.5 × 1 cm/2 × 1 × ½ in	19.2	1.8	137
Parmesan, grated	5	1 level teaspoon	1.6	0.2	20
Processed cheese	45	5 × 2.5 × 1 cm/2 × 1 × ½ in *or* 1½ individually wrapped slices	26.6	1.0	140
Stilton	45	5 × 2.5 × 1 cm/2 × 1 × ½ in	22.5	1.8	208
Butter, salted	5	1 level teaspoon	1.9	Tr	37
Butter, unsalted	5	1 level teaspoon	Tr	Tr	37
Cream, double	15	1 tablespoon	0.2	0.3	67
Cream, single	15	1 tablespoon	0.3	0.5	32
Egg	50	1 medium	3.0	1.8	74
Margarine, salted	5	1 level teaspoon	1.7	Tr	36
Margarine, unsalted	5	1 level teaspoon	Tr	Tr	36
Milk, goat's	200	1 cup	3.5	9.2	142
Milk, whole	200	1 cup	4.4	7.7	130
Milk, skimmed	200	1 cup	4.4	7.7	66
Vegetable oil	15	1 tablespoon	Tr	Tr	135
Yoghurt, plain	150	¾ cup	5.0	9.2	78
Yoghurt, flavoured	150	¾ cup	4.2	8.5	122

Bread, biscuits, cakes, cereals

	Wt (g)	Handy measure	Sodium mmol	Potassium mmol	Kcal
Bread					
Bread, brown	40	1 slice	9.6	2.2	89
Bread, salt-free white	40	1 slice	0.1	1.0	93
Bread, salt-free wholemeal	40	1 slice	0.1	2.3	86
Bread, white	40	1 slice	9.4	1.0	93
Bread, wholemeal	40	1 slice	9.4	2.3	86
Chapati	120	1 × 18 cm/7 in, thin	6.3	4.6	242
Pizza, cheese and tomato, salt added	120	Individual, 15 cm/6 in diameter	17.7	5.5	281

	Wt (g)	Handy measure	Sodium mmol	Potassium mmol	Kcal
Roll, brown	40	1 roll	11.0	2.4	114
Roll, white	40	1 roll	11.0	1.2	107
Biscuits					
Biscuit, chocolate-covered	21	1	1.7	1.4	126
Biscuit, cream filled	10	1	1.0	0.3	51
Biscuit, digestive	15	1	2.9	0.6	71
Biscuit, semi-sweet	16	2	2.8	0.6	73
Cream crackers	15	2	4.0	0.5	66
Crispbread, rye	16	2	1.5	2.0	51
Oatcake	12	1	6.4	1.0	53
Cakes and puddings					
Cake, rich fruit, no icing	80	2.5 × 3.5 × 6 cm/ 1 × 1½ × 2½ in	5.9	8.8	266
Cake, rich fruit, marzipan and icing	100	2.5 × 3.5 × 6 cm/ 1 × 1½ × 3 in	5.2	9.2	352
Cake, victoria sponge, no icing	55	⅙ of 18 cm/7 in diameter cake	8.4	1.2	255
Cheesecake	130	¼ of 18 cm/7 in diameter cake	14.7	4.0	547
Custard sauce, made with powder	150	¾ cup	5.0	6.5	177
Doughnut, jam filled	75	1	2.0	2.1	262
Fruit crumble	100	7 × 7 cm/3 × 3 in portion	4.8	4.4	208
Fruit pie	75	small individual, 7 cm/ 3 in wide	6.8	2.3	277
Ice cream	50	small slice, 1 cm/½ in wide ·	1.6	2.1	83
Jam tart	50	1 individual	5.0	1.4	182
Jelly, made up	150	2 heaped tablespoons	0.4	0.2	88
Milk pudding	200	1 cup	4.8	8.2	262
Pancake	50	20 cm/8 in diameter, thin	1.1	1.8	154
Pastry, salt added	80	8 × 8 cm/3½ in square	13.2	1.6	353
Scone, white, salt added	35	1 medium	12.2	1.3	130
Sponge pudding, steamed	100	8 × 8 × 3.5 cm/ 3 × 3 × 1½ in	13.5	2.3	340
Trifle	120	2 heaped tablespoons	2.6	4.6	192
Yorkshire pudding, salt added	15	1 small individual	3.9	0.6	32
Cereals					
Bran, wheat	5	1 level tablespoon	0.1	1.5	10
Cornflour	15	1 level tablespoon	0.3	0.2	53
Custard powder	15	1 level tablespoon	2.1	0.2	53
Flour, brown 100%	30	1 rounded tablespoon	Tr	32.9	98

	Wt (g)	Handy measure	Sodium mmol	Potassium mmol	Kcal
Flour, white, plain	30	1 rounded tablespoon	Tr	1.1	105
Flour white, self-raising	30	1 rounded tablespoon	4.6	1.3	102
Flour, wholemeal 100%	30	1 rounded tablespoon	Tr	2.8	95
Macaroni, white, boiled	120	1 cup	0.4	2.1	140
Macaroni, wholemeal, boiled*	120	1 cup	0.1	3.8	123
Oatmeal, dry	30	½ cup	0.4	2.8	120
Porridge, made with salt and water	200	1 cup	50.4	2.2	88
Rice, brown, boiled*	120	3 heaped tablespoons	0.1	1.8	120
Rice, white, boiled	120	3 heaped tablespoons	0.1	1.2	148
Spaghetti, canned in tomato sauce	200	1 cup	43.5	6.7	118
Spaghetti, white, boiled	120	1 cup	0.3	1.4	140
Spaghetti, wholemeal, boiled	120	1 cup	0.1	3.8	123

Breakfast cereals

	Wt (g)	Handy measure	Sodium mmol	Potassium mmol	Kcal
All-Bran	60	1 cup	43.6	16.5	164
Cornflakes	30	1 cup	15.1	0.8	110
Muesli, bought	50	5 level tablespoons	3.9	7.7	184
Puffed Wheat	30	6 rounded tablespoons	Tr	3.0	98
Rice Krispies	30	1 cup	14.5	1.2	117
Shredded Wheat	23	1 biscuit	0.1	2.0	74
Sugar Puffs	30	6 rounded tablespoons	0.1	1.2	104

Nuts

	Wt (g)	Handy measure	Sodium mmol	Potassium mmol	Kcal
Almonds, shelled	30	1 heaped tablespoon	0.1	6.6	170
Brazils, shelled	15	4	Tr	2.9	93
Chestnuts, shelled	30	4	0.1	3.8	51
Cob/Hazelnuts, shelled	25	1 heaped tablespoon	Tr	2.2	95
Coconut	15	5 × 5 cm/2 × 2 in piece	0.1	1.7	53
Peanut, butter	10	1 rounded teaspoon	1.5	1.8	62
Peanuts, fresh	30	2 level tablespoons	0.1	5.2	171
Peanuts, salted	30	2 level tablespoons	5.7	5.2	171
Walnuts, shelled	25	1 heaped tablespoon	Tr	2.8	131

*Not McCance and Widdowson's figures

Sauces and pickles

NB These items are all shop-bought, not homemade.

	Wt (g)	*Handy measure*	Sodium mmol	Potassium mmol	Kcal
Brown sauce	15	1 level tablespoon	6.4	1.5	15
Chutney, apple	15	1 level tablespoon	0.8	1.2	23
Mayonnaise	15	1 level tablespoon	2.3	0.1	108
Piccalilli	15	1 level tablespoon	2.6	0.1	5
Pickle, sweet	15	1 level tablespoon	11.1	0.4	20
Salad cream	15	1 level tablespoon	5.5	0.3	47
Soy sauce*	5	1 level teaspoon	16.0	0.5	Neg
Tomato ketchup	15	1 level tablespoon	7.3	2.3	15
Tomato purée with salt	5	1 level teaspoon	0.9	2.0	3

Soups

	Wt (g)	*Handy measure*	Sodium mmol	Potassium mmol	Kcal
Chicken, cream of	200	1 cup	40.0	2.1	116
Chicken noodle	200	1 cup	32.0	0.8	40
Lentil	200	1 cup	16.0	8.2	198
Minestrone	200	1 cup	37.0	3.2	46
Mushroom, cream of	200	1 cup	41.0	2.8	106
Oxtail	200	1 cup	38.0	4.8	88
Tomato, cream of	200	1 cup	40.0	9.7	110
Vegetable	200	1 cup	43.0	7.2	74

Cooking ingredients

	Wt (g)	*Handy measure*	Sodium mmol	Potassium mmol	Kcal
Baking powder	2.5	1 level teaspoon	12.8	Tr	4
Bovril	5	1 level teaspoon	10.4	1.5	9
Curry powder	3	1 level teaspoon	0.6	1.4	7
Marmite	5	1 level teaspoon	9.8	3.3	9
Oxo cube	6	1 cube	26.9	1.1	14
Salt	5	1 level teaspoon	84.4	Tr	0
Vinegar	5	1 teaspoon	Tr	0.1	Tr
Yeast, dried	4	1 level teaspoon	0.1	2.0	6

*Not McCance and Widdowson's figures

Beverages

	Wt (g)	Handy measure	Sodium mmol	Potassium mmol	Kcal
Cocoa powder	3	1 rounded teaspoon	1.2	1.2	9
Coffee, ground, infusion	200	1 cup	Tr	3.4	4
Coffee, instant	2	1 slightly rounded teaspoon	Tr	2.0	2
Drinking chocolate	10	2 heaped teaspoons	1.1	1.0	37
Horlicks	10	2 heaped teaspoons	1.5	1.9	40
Ovaltine	10	2 heaped teaspoons	0.6	2.2	38
Tea, infusion	200	1 cup	Tr	0.9	Tr
Soft drinks and juices					
Coca-Cola	200	1 cup	0.7	Tr	78
Grapefruit juice, unsweetened	200	1 cup	0.3	5.6	62
Lemonade, bottled	200	1 cup	0.6	Tr	42
Lime juice cordial	30	2 tablespoons	0.1	0.4	34
Lucozade	200	1 cup	2.5	Tr	136
Orange drink, undiluted	30	2 tablespoons	0.3	0.1	32
Orange juice, unsweetened	200	1 cup	0.3	6.7	66
Pineapple juice	200	1 cup	0.1	7.2	106
Ribena	30	2 tablespoons	0.3	0.7	69
Tomato juice	200	1 cup	20.0	13.3	32

Sugar, conserves, confectionery

	Wt (g)	Handy measure	Sodium mmol	Potassium mmol	Kcal
Boiled sweets	5	1	Tr	Tr	16
Chocolate, milk	50	1 small bar	2.6	5.4	264
Chocolate, plain	50	1 small bar	0.2	3.8	262
Chocolates, fancy	15	1	0.4	0.9	69
Honey	5	1 level teaspoon	Tr	0.1	14
Jam	5	1 level teaspoon	Tr	0.1	13
Marmalade	5	1 level teaspoon	Tr	0.1	13
Marzipan	15	2.5 × 2.5 × 1 cm/ 1 × 1 × ½ in piece	0.1	1.5	66
Peppermints	5	1	Tr	Tr	20
Sugar, demerara	5	1 rounded teaspoon	Tr	0.1	20
Sugar, white	5	1 rounded teaspoon	Tr	0.0	20
Syrup, golden	5	1 level teaspoon	0.6	0.3	15
Toffee	10	1	1.4	0.5	43
Treacle, black	5	1 level teaspoon	0.2	1.9	13

Alcoholic drinks

	Wt (g)	Handy measure	Sodium mmol	Potassium mmol	Kcal
Beers					
Brown ale, bottled	300	0.25 litre/½ pint (1 small bottle)	2.1	2.5	84
Canned beer, bitter	300	0.25 litre/½ pint (1 small can)	1.2	2.8	96
Draught bitter	300	0.25 litre/½ pint (1 glass)	1.6	2.9	96
Keg bitter	300	0.25 litre/½ pint (1 glass)	1.0	2.7	93
Lager, bottled	300	0.25 litre/½ pint (1 small bottle)	0.5	2.6	87
Stout, bottled	300	0.25 litre/½ pint (1 small bottle)	3.0	3.5	111
Stout, extra	300	0.25 litre/½ pint (1 glass)	0.5	6.6	117
Strong ale	300	0.25 litre/½ pint (1 glass)	2.0	8.5	216
Cider, dry	300	0.25 litre/½ pint (1 glass)	0.9	5.5	108
Cider, sweet	300	0.25 litre/½ pint (1 glass)	0.9	5.5	126
Wines and fortified wines					
Red wine	150	1 glass (¹/₅ bottle)	0.6	5.0	102
Rosé, medium	150	1 glass (¹/₅ bottle)	0.3	2.9	106
White wine, dry	150	1 glass (¹/₅ bottle)	0.3	2.4	99
White wine, medium	150	1 glass (¹/₅ bottle)	1.4	3.4	112
White wine, sweet	150	1 glass (¹/₅ bottle)	0.8	4.2	141
White wine, sparkling	150	1 glass (¹/₅ bottle)	0.3	2.2	114
Port	100	½ cup	0.2	2.5	157
Sherry, medium	50	¼ cup	0.1	1.1	59
Vermouth, dry	50	¼ cup	0.4	0.5	59
Vermouth, sweet	50	¼ cup	0.6	0.4	76
Spirits					
(70 per cent proof)	25	1 measure, approximately 2 tablespoons	Tr	Tr	56

ACKNOWLEDGEMENTS

I am very grateful to Marie Roberts, formerly Blood Pressure and Metabolic Unit dietitian at Charing Cross Hospital, who provided all the calculations and tables as well as much advice.

Many others in the Blood Pressure Unit at Charing Cross Hospital and St George's Hospital have helped me and I am indebted to all of them, particularly Diana Elder and Nirmala Markandu.

Graham MacGregor, 1990

The publishers are grateful to the following individuals and organisations for their help in the preparation of this book. Revlon Health Care (UK) for their assistance with the photographs; David Mellor Ltd, 26 James Street, WC2 for providing some of the kitchen equpiment.

The photographs were taken by Peter Myers, assisted by Neil Mersh; art direction was by Rose and Lamb Design Partnership, styling by Penny Markham and food preparation by Lisa Collard.

The diagrams were drawn by David Gifford.

INDEX

Other titles in the series

HIGH BLOOD PRESSURE
What it means for you, and how to control it
Dr Eoin O'Brien and
Prof Kevin O'Malley

BEAT HEART DISEASE!
A cardiologist explains how you can help your heart and enjoy a healthier life
Prof Risteard Mulcahy

DON'T FORGET FIBRE IN YOUR DIET
To help avoid many of our commonest diseases
Dr Denis Burkitt

ASTHMA AND HAY FEVER
How to relieve wheezing and sneezing
Dr Allan Knight

OVERCOMING ARTHRITIS
A guide to coping with stiff or aching joints
Dr Frank Dudley Hart

PSORIASIS
A guide to one of the commonest skin diseases
Prof Ronald Marks

DIABETES
A practical guide to healthy living
Dr Jim Anderson

THE DIABETICS' DIET BOOK
A new high-fibre eating programme
Dr Jim Mann and the Oxford Dietetic Group

STRESS AND RELAXATION
Self-help ways to cope with stress and relieve nervous tension, ulcers, insomnia, migraine and high blood-pressure
Jane Madders

VARICOSE VEINS
How they are treated, and what you can do to help
Prof Harold Ellis

ECZEMA AND DERMATITIS
How to cope with inflamed skin
Prof Rona MacKie

ANXIETY AND DEPRESSION
A practical guide to recovery
Prof Robert Priest

ACNE
Advice on clearing your skin
Prof Ronald Marks

OVERCOMING DYSLEXIA
A straightforward guide for families and teachers
Dr Bevé Hornsby

EYES
Their problems and treatments
Michael Glasspool, FRCS

CONQUERING PAIN
How to overcome the discomfort of arthritis, backache, migraine, heart disease, childbirth, period pains and many other common conditions
Dr Sampson Lipton

THE DIABETICS' COOKBOOK
Delicious new recipes for entertaining and all the family
Roberta Longstaff, SRD,
and Dr Jim Mann